Get Married... STAY MARRIED

Keys to building and keeping your marriage

ADEREMI BADRU

All Scriptures, unless otherwise stated are from The Authorized (King James) Version. Rights in the Authorized Version in the United Kingdom are vested in the Crown. Reproduced by permission of the Crown's patentee, Cambridge University Press

Get Married, Stay Married
Copyright ©2017 by Aderemi Badru
ISBN: 978-1-908243-06-5

Published by
The Base Media
8 Jessop Court, The Alders,
Morriston, Swansea. SA6 6PS
www.thebasemedia.com

Printed in the United Kingdom
All rights reserved. No part of this publication may be reproduced, stored in a retrieval system, or transmitted, in any form or by any means, electronic, mechanical, photocopying, recording or otherwise, without the prior permission of the publisher, except for the inclusion of brief quotations in a review.

Dedication

I dedicate this book to my Priceless Jewel "Oluwatobiloba" for your love, support and commitment to our marriage and ministry has enabled me to learn the truths shared in this book and has helped made me a man after God's heart.

I also dedicate this book to all the young men and women out there who are struggling in their marital relationships but have determined to keep working until their marital relationships becomes a heaven on earth.

Finally, I dedicate this book to my spiritual children in Nigeria and the members of The Rebuilders' Ministries International who keep pressing me to put together a material that will help the next generation build godly and lasting homes. Thank you for always believing in me. I love you all deeply!

Acknowledgement

Writing and Publishing this book is possible because God inspired me, enabled me and provided all that is needed, for which I am grateful to Him. I also appreciate the efforts of all those that contributed in typing, arranging and editing. The counsel, contributions and recommendations of Dr & Mrs Samson Omotosho, Pastor Yemi Hamid Oke, Rev Dr. Anderson (Colonial Baptist Church, Randallstown, Maryland), Rev. Dr Michael Salim Mattar (Director of Missions and Church Planter, Montgomery Baptist Association, Montgomery County, Maryland), Pastor Bukky Gbenro (The Vineyard Assembly, Ibadan, Oyo State, Nigeria) and Pastor Ebenezer Diyaolu (Lagos) is highly appreciated. I appreciate the commitment of Pastor Felix Makanjuola Jr. (Swansea, United Kingdom), for the book design, layout and the concept. Lastly, I cannot but appreciate the effort of my Priceless Jewel in ensuring that this book is a success.

Remarks About The Book

In a day of increasing marital breakdown, this book by Aderemi Badru re-establishes the Biblical truth regarding marriage. Pastor Badru presents a thorough and solid understanding of what God meant when He created the institution of marriage. The author addresses many problems going into and stay within the marriage relationship, and Badru is both practical and insightful in discussing these various concerns. This is a must read for those planning to marry, as well as those desiring to stay married! You will not regret having this book at your fingertips."

Dr. Robert J. Anderson, Jr.
Colonial Baptist Church, Randallstown, MD.

This is another reason why I believe Rev. Aderemi Badru would make an effective professional Marriage and Family Counsellor! He has put together a book on marriage that will be of tremendous help to young couples, those contemplating marriage, and those that desire to make their particular marriages healthier and successful. The book has touched on many important knotty issues and challenges that husbands and wives confront on a day to day basis. Based on Christian principles, the book provides practical lessons for anyone seeking wisdom to make their marriage one that brings satisfaction and pleasure both to them and to God. Good job!

Prof. Samson Omotosho.
Program Director; Optimum Health Systems, Inc. Baltimore, MD.

"But you, go your way till the end; for you shall rest and will arise to your inheritance at the end of the days" Daniel 12:13. The beauty of any journey is not to start but to get to the end successfully. Marital relationship is a journey of destiny. Pastor Remi has passionately chatted a map for a safe journey in marriage from the word of God. I recommend this book highly to everyone hoping to navigate the corridor of marriage and those who love them.

Bukki Gbenro,
TVA, Inc., Ibadan, Oyo State, Nigeria

This book from Rev Aderemi Badru is both captivating and inspiring. It is useful for both the singles and the married. This book has combined sound biblical teaching on marriage with practical illustrations that will help the reader to understand the purpose of God for marriage and to enjoy the bliss of marriage. I therefore recommend this book to everyone whose desire is to get married and stay married.

Ebenezer Diyaolu,
Family Care Mandate, International.

Contents

Dedication 3
Acknowledgment..5
Remarks about the book 7
Read this First 11
Chapter   I - So You Are Getting Married 15
Chapter II - Why Do You Want to Get Married?.... 35
Chapter III - Excuse Me, Who Do I Marry? 49
Chapter IV- Now That You Are Married! 87
Chapter V - This Bride and Her Groom.................99
Chapter VI - It is Time to Be the Groom
                    and the Husband. 115
Chapter VII - Are You Ready to Be the Wife 127
Chapter VIII - Two Shall Become One.................149
Chapter IX - Naked and Not Ashamed 167
Chapter X - I hate Divorce..................................187
Chapter XI - The Fire Must Not Go Out 225
Bibliography/Scripture Index............................257

Read This First

How excited are you about getting married? In a world where marriage has been redefined, a lot of people approach marriage with fear. It is true that so many people have great misunderstandings and erroneous beliefs about marriage which they have formed from the various experiences of people around them. In my interactions with a lot of young people, I discovered that many of them see marriage as a bondage while others have mixed feelings about it. Someone once said that "marriage is like a bottle of honey; the flies outside are dying to come in, while the ones inside are dying to go out".

Nevertheless, we must come to the point when we can accurately define marriage as God the initiator defines it and that is what this book is aimed at achieving. It is not a fable that "when the purpose of something is not known, abuse will be inevitable". There is no way a man can succeed in what he has no knowledge of and has concluded even before going into it that it will fail. This is a fundamental problem that I see with so many people coming into marriage, many have concluded that it will fail even before it started. Did Job say in vain that "what I fear has happened to me"? It is not just a Christian principle that we are all products of our thoughts and faith. How do you explain that "some people see marriage as a chewing gum, that when you start to chew, it's so sweet with a lot of sugar, but the more you chew, the more sugar reduces and mere rubber remains until you feel like spewing it out"? That mind-set of marriage is a mind-set that will lead to failure because that is not in alignment with the word of God and God's purpose for marriage.

In our world today, in America, Africa, Asia and other parts of the world, the devil is busy fighting the institution of marriage. He is busy doing what he knows best to do; he is busy stealing, killing and destroying homes and many people are falling prey to him. This must not happen to you, your marriage must not join the list of failed marriages; your marriage was purposed by God to be a heaven on earth and not the hell that the devil is painting it for people all over the world.

This book was inspired by the Holy Spirit to help you understand the counsel and mind of God on marriage and the principles to make it work. This book is not based on just the experiences of people but is based on the authority and the efficacy of the word of God. One common thing that has been misleading a lot of young people is the negative experience of people that surround them. This book is both useful for those who are intending to get married and those who are already married. You can be sure that there will definitely be human errors in one way or the other, but I hope that you can set your mind on the message that God will be bringing to you through this book. I believe that your marriage will work and that your home will be a heaven on earth. Thanks for reading.

Your friend,
Aderemi Badru

Chapter 1

So You Are Getting Married?

I remember the day I called mama on the telephone. I told her, mama, I'm getting married. I could hear her voice from the other side of the telephone; she was smiling. And she asked me a question that I proudly answered. She said son, did you take time to know her? I said mama she is the best. But today it hurts me so badly, to go to mama and say mama, I'm getting divorced. Oh, I'm getting divorced. This choice I made didn't work out the way I thought it would; it hurts me so mama. Mama said to me, it's not easy to understand it son but I hope you'll make it. You'll be happy again. I remember in church, when the preacher read the scriptures, you looked so beautiful and innocent. I didn't know that behind the beauty lies the true colour that will destroy me in the nearest future. I remember when I held you by the hand while the preacher man read the scriptures, putting words in your mouth. Maybe what the preacher man said was not something that was within you. Now I know what they mean when they say beautiful woman is another man's plaything. Oh lord, I am hurting now; this choice I made didn't work out the way I thought it would'.

- LUCKY DUBE

It's a beautiful Saturday morning, the day is just breaking. Friends and family members have travelled several distances to celebrate this day with me. Yes, it is my wedding day! I cannot hide the excitement I feel because this is a day that I have longed for and now my parents can be proud of me. My phones are buzzing with congratulatory messages and calls; everyone seems to be happy for me. Of course, the truth is that I was awake all night waiting for today to arrive. The caterers are so busy with preparing meals for the day, the reception hall is being prepared for a beautiful ceremony and all that remains is for me to get ready for church so that I can be joined with my sweetheart and we can become husband and wife and live in joy and happiness for the rest of our lives.

I was in this mood of joy and excitement, when my phone began to ring. I razed to pick it and lo, it was my dear friend who was calling to congratulate me; but the first statement he made changed my mood and caused me to sit down and ponder again about the decision I was about to take. He said, "Ore (i.e. Friend), so you are getting married? I am so happy for you and I pray that God bless your marriage". It was that moment that I realized that I was getting married and not just that I was going to have a ceremony. Does that mean that I did not know before that time that I was preparing to get married? In utmost sincerity, the excitement of the occasion and the need for preparation had not allowed me to ponder deeply on the reality that I was about to go into.

As I dropped the phone, I remembered our last counselling session with the pastor of the church where we were to get married. I remember that as he was rounding off that session with us, he asked us if we were aware of the implications of our decision to get married. He also told us to realize that from the moment we got married everything would change and we must never forget that. How would I explain my feelings from that moment? Would I call it fear? Would I call it sorrow or doubts? All I can say is that from that moment, my excitements died down and the reality of the truth that I was getting married began to dawn on me. It was just a few hours to the wedding ceremony and everyone was getting ready for this occasion but there I was thinking about the decision that I was about to take, which I was sure will change my life forever. All I could do at that point was go on my knees and pray, pleading with God to help me on this journey to an unknown destination that I was about to enter into.

In church, the pastor was leading the congregation and charging us to know the purpose of marriage; my heart began to beat faster when he got to the point when he said, "marriage is a holy estate that God ordained himself and this holy estate must not be entered into unadvisedly, impatiently and without being sure." I know I loved the person I was about to get married to, but did I really understand everything I needed to understand about this institution I was about to enter into was the question on my mind. I took my time to underline every statement that the pastor made on the purpose of marriage and I decided to study it thereafter.

At about 1:05 pm, the pastor asked, "do you take this person as your lawful wedded husband, to hold, to love, to cherish, in sickness, in health, in riches, in poverty and in all things till death do you part?" I watched her say, "I do, so help me God", so at that juncture I knew that most of the people that have said I do in times past really did not understand to what they said "I do" to and that is why it was easy for them to break up or divorce with someone they had pledged to stick with till death do them part. It was my turn to say I do, but since I know that God was the number one witness to my marriage and then the thousands of people that were there to celebrate with us, I decided to say I do with utmost conviction; so when the preacher asked me, I said 'I do' but I also said within myself that yes I do even if I really don't understand to what I was saying, "yes, I do".

Is that story familiar to you? Do you know that several people walked to the altar today to be solemnized in what we call holy matrimony? But do you also know that many of those people that took that great decision never had an idea of what they were going into? Someone once told me that marriage is a black market where you do not know what you are buying until you get home, but I disagree with him. It is so funny to hear people say that if I have known what is in marriage I would not have gone into it. I really do not know why we are so used to blaming people and things for the things we ought to take responsibility for.

The song of regret is the song that many people seem to be singing in their marriages and you wonder why. Why is it that so many people in marriage are praying to be divorced? Divorce lawyers are so busy these days and even marriages that were solemnised in the church are breaking up in terrifying rates. A public notary asked me recently why pastors seems not to be paying attention to the issue of high rates of divorce in the society, most especially among Christians. It is so pathetic that the couples that once sang love songs for each other are now beating drums of war in their homes every day. The most painful part of this issue is that in recent times the news of couples murdering each other in cold blood seems to be on a high increase everywhere I have turned to. Why? Is it God's fault?

The wedding service is about to begin; people are gathered into the sanctuary with an air of expectancy; a popular couple from the church is about to commit to each other for the rest of their lives. They have gone together for the past three years and everyone in the church sees them as a perfect match, intelligent, expressive, and fervently serving the Lord in the church. But who would have thought that just after three years, this couple will be meeting in a court room to dissolve their marriage? **Does it not bother you that love stories are turning into tales of death and sorrow?** A young woman said to her pastor recently in his office, "when I got married, I was looking for an ideal but I married an ordeal and now I want a new deal." Is it God's fault? Is there a way we can determine if someone is ready for marriage or not?

Young people these days do not want to get married; the experiences of marital failure that they see all around is simply enough to scare them and make them see marriage as an evil in disguise, when God ordained it to be a blessing. It is embarrassing to hear different reasons why so many people are breaking up their marriages, including pastors and ministers of God. Is there a spiritual attack on marriages by the devil or is there something we are not doing right? While couples are breaking up, the children from such homes are thrown into life gloom and darkness. They are left torn between two worlds and they are made to see a world of violence and evil. My friend, I do not intend to blame the couples who are breaking up but rather to take you through what the Lord has helped me to discover as the ultimate reason that many people are having tough times in their marriage. So if you are getting married, let's look at these issues together.

This is not Hollywood!

Actors are paid to act and that is what they do professionally. They have scripts written for them to act and roles given to them to interpret. No matter what role an actor or actress plays in a movie, you will be a fool to conclude that that is who he or she is in reality. I spent some time recently with a popular drama minister in Nigeria and I discovered that he was so shy and that contradicts what I used to see of him in his movies. Nevertheless, **it is shameful that my generation has allowed what they see in movies to define for them the realities of life**. Marriages in the movies are the exact opposite of what a godly marriage should be in reality and I am beginning to feel that most of the actors and actresses that are involved in these movies are beginning to manifest the errors that we see in their movies. What we see is more of false living, vague lives and pretence among these actors and actresses. Will it not be painful for someone to interpret an acting role as his role in life?

Hence, I see a generation of young people who are daily patterning their lives on what they see in the movies and in films. While, I do not intend to condemn the movie industry, I believe that the time has come for us to emphasize to this generation that **there is a vast difference between what is seen on the television and what the reality of life is**. It is sad that many parents have not paid attention to teaching their children, thereby allowing Hollywood, Bollywood and Nollywood to teach them. The church of Christ in the end time has also failed to teach the next generation what the word of God says on salient issues especially marriage. Rather, they are allowing the movie industry to define and deform our world with lies.

What does God say about marriage? Whose idea was marriage? Does anyone have the right to define what he does not understand as his purpose? The movie industry has reduced marriage to an institution where people have sex. The picture that is always painted is that of a young man and woman meeting in an awkward situation, then fall in love and begin to have sex, visit parks and eateries. The next thing is that they are seen living together and then later, they will decide to see their parents. All of these movies helped in spreading errors about cohabitation, what love is, and sex as a true demonstration or proof of love. **It brings tears to my eyes when I see our youths actually translating what they see in movies into their daily living and are later left to lick their wounds**. No blame on the movie industry. They are simply doing their job.

Does it not bother you that most of the actors and the actresses in those movies are not comfortably settled in marriages of their own; while many of them try to cover up by saying that they do not want to be married for several reasons ranging from career to the desire for independence, yet there is a vacuum that many of them are longing to fill. I enjoy watching movies but our lives cannot be patterned after them. **God's word is the standard and that is why most of the issues that will be raised in this book will be treated from the scriptural perspective.** We are not in the movies. Movies are acted for entertainment, conscious and unconscious instructions for viewers, business for the producer and the actors and actresses. So whatever is seen in them is not real, although some of them are acted, based on real life events. There are movies that instruct us and warn us about life consequences, but no matter what, our lives cannot be built on 'acts'; life is more real than that.

The Error

It is the level of our preparation that determines the level of success that we will attain in life. If people prepare so hard for success in other things, why then do we think we do not need to prepare for marriage. It is funny that we spend so much energy and time to prepare for the wedding events but we pay little or no attention to the realities in marriage. Does this not explain to us why so many marriages are not working? **Many people that came into marriage never prepared themselves for this lifelong important decision.** We have even come to the era when event planners are busy planning wedding for people who are not prepared themselves for the journey they are embarking on. How can someone embark on a journey without having an idea of the destination and the route to follow to get there? **Is it then not an error for someone to then join himself with another on a life long journey without having a thorough understanding of where they are going, how they will get there and what the journey entails?**

The list of people that have become casualties on this journey called marriage is becoming longer day by day, yet is it not foolish for you not to prepare yourself for the same journey? Why do so many people end up regretting when it is too late, when they could have prevented and averted the dangers that they see happening around them? Animals without common sense pay attention to danger signs when they see it and they flee; but we humans often keep travelling to the same place where the danger signals are evident. This is the error and that is what I intend to help you avoid in this book.

God wants you to enjoy your marriage just like I have said earlier and he wants your marriage to make you better in life and not bitter. Your marriage should enhance your fulfilling destiny and make you both efficient and effective in life; it is not the other way round that the society and the devil keep painting it. The fear of failure is what is keeping so many people away from marriage instead of them getting themselves prepared to enjoy the bliss. Lack of preparation is synonymous to failure in anything. **You should not expect God to do for you the things you need to do for yourself. He will do his part and you have to do your part.** You need to use all the opportunities that you and I have to prepare ourselves for the marital journey, after all some people never had the opportunity of even reading a book to enlighten them on marriage.

The blame game has been going on for so long. We might have inherited that from Adam and Eve; it was Eve that Adam blamed for his errors when God confronted him and Eve turned to the snake as an excuse for her error. It did not work because none of them were willing to even own up to the fact that they had sinned, so God sent them out of the garden of pleasure. You do not need to look for whom to blame later, because no one will be responsible to live your life for you and that is why I counsel that you prepare well for your future home.

Why are you afraid?

A movie star in Nigeria was interviewed recently. She was asked why she had refused to get married at her age. She had a daughter, but she preferred living as a single mother. She told the reporters that she had chosen not to get married because she was afraid of divorce. Isn't she truthful? She is, and she has expressed the opinions of so many young people out there. She has succumbed to fear and she has allowed the fear of failure that she has seen in other people's marriage to tailor her mind-set and expectations about marriage. **Fear is nothing but a weapon that is used by the devil to enslave people.** He has three instruments that he uses which are manipulation, intimidation and domination. Fear has been defined as false experience appearing real. It is just like someone running away from his shadows. Fear has kept a lot of people in bondage and it comes along with torment. **So many people are living out their fears instead of fulfilling their dreams.**

A friend was sharing with me recently on how scared he is of getting into any relationship; he does not have problems with meeting wonderful and marriageable ladies but he has been in bondage of fear all along. His fear actually grew from the negative words that were spoken into his life as a child where he grew from and this has affected his self-confidence which is now negatively impacting his marital desires. Many people are suffering from fear as a result of various negative experiences of life either that they were involved in directly or that they witness happen to people around them. It is often impossible to see beyond our fears if we cannot deal with it based on the truth that we know. It is our ability to live beyond fear that gives us the capacity to enjoy our lives. On daily basis we are all faced with situations that scare us and fear is a constant factor in everyone but how we react and respond to it is what determines if we will be able to make the best of it.

The example of my friend described above is just one out of many of people who are not even confident of taking the decision to get married because of the damage that was done to them emotionally and psychologically as children. **When**

children grow up in a negative environment, they tend to live in negativity all their lives. We are all a product of our environment or background and no matter how much we try; we still show signs of what we inherited from our growing up experiences. Nevertheless, we must be ready to rise beyond these limitations because it has the capacity to crush our hopes and aspirations for life. **Children who grew up seeing their parents constantly fighting each other might live with the fear of not wanting to experience that same experience, so they may choose not to get married**. It is unfortunate that parents do not realise the extent of damage that they do to their children as they grow up seeing them in negativity. I am still dealing with a case of a child who saw his father threw her mother inside the water to drown; as a result, the mother lost her sight. This young lady hence has decided never to marry and she sees men as evil. Is she not justified? Yes, she may be, but she must rise above it to enjoy the fullness of life that God has purposed for her.

It is strange to see how many women are woman-right fighters today or feminists because of the horrible experience that they saw their mothers go through in the hands of their fathers; they are thus leading people into error, judging every one by their pains. I feel their pains but they must come out of it and use it to their advantage. **Sometimes, professional help may be needed to fully heal such deep-seated emotional trauma and there are**

good Christian Marriage and Family Counsellors who offer such help. Fear will keep you perpetually down and never allow you to truly succeed. I heard of a family where the father in anger poured a pot of hot rice on the wife in the presence of the children and till today the woman's head cannot grow hair. What will you say to such children when it comes to marriage? Yes, that fear alone can keep them from getting married but honestly they must not allow it. I grew up in fear too but I decided to have a home that is a heaven on earth which is contrary to what my parents had. Sometimes you just have to decide that your experience will be different.

Child abuse and rape is another cause for fear in a lot of people about marriage. It has been revealed that many people who have been abused in one way or the other often live in that fear and ultimately it affects their relationship with other people. A lady who was sexually abused by her father once told me of how much anger and resentment she has towards men; so for her, marriage is a no go area. I have seen terrible things in my relationship with the young people in the last seven years and it is sometimes difficult to convince them to see beyond their predicaments. **Nevertheless, there is healing in Jesus because there is a balm in Gilead and that is our message to anyone been tormented by fear.** What fear does to people is to torment them using their past experiences and the experiences of other people around them to limit them from excelling in life.

Fear must be dealt with before anyone walk into marriage because if it is not, the marriage will be short lived. As I said earlier, sometimes professional help may be needed to fully treat such deep-seated fear and trauma and there are good Christian Marriage and Family Counsellors who can help.

As a secondary school student back then, many of us were made to believe that every one that writes the senior secondary school certificate examination fails Mathematics and English. No one really told us that some other students who wrote the examination passed those two subjects in flying colours. So, fear of Mathematics and English was instilled in all of us waiting to write the examination. I ended up failing the examination too because I had already concluded that I will fail since others failed. I judged my own expectation based on their failures. Is that not what many of us are doing? We are using the experiences of people that have failed around us to conclude our own lives. Is that not the reason many people are even scared of marriage?

It is possible that your parents do not enjoy a beautiful marriage, but that is not a yardstick for your own future marriage. Do not judge your own marriage based on the experience of other people around you who are failing. Your fear attracts to you what you experience in life. Job said, 'what I have feared has eventually happened to me (Job 3:25)'. **Fear is a strong magnetic force that attracts to us our negative expectations.** Marriage is not evil like the devil wants you to believe. In fact, **the devil is**

the one that is afraid of your marriage because he knows if you marry rightly, then you will produce godly seeds that will destroy his kingdom. He hates unity, love and truth and that is why he is desperately doing everything possible to keep you from enjoying the best God has for you in marriage.

You must not let fear rob you of the joy in marriage. It is truly regrettable that many of us have gone through some damaging experiences but we must find wholeness and hope in the fact that there are others who have gone through what we are going through and they are successfully married. We must find strength to live in the midst of these tormenting fears and heart breaking pains which we can only do through putting our trust in Jesus. We cannot afford to remain as slaves to our past. Yes, what happened to you is evil but it can become a testimony if you see beyond the negative impact. Do not let your mind be damaged towards marriage; God intends that you find wholeness, help and comfort in marriage. You must also be ready to reach out to people that can help you; open up on those issues, that is definitely a sure way to recovery. Until you are able to talk about those experiences, you might find it difficult to really experience wholeness. Speak out and let God use people to help you heal up.

Marriage is beautiful, it is not bondage!

God in his word made it clear that He instituted marriage to correct a deficiency in man's life. All the things that He made was declared good (perfect), but the same God saw that the man he had created in His own image lacked something crucial which will make his life incomplete. "It is not good that the man should not be alone" says the Lord. What an observation! In God's love, he saw that man lacked a companion and a helper, so God decided to make Eve. The above narration may not be quoted the way it was written in the scriptures (Genesis 2:18) but it has been carefully explained to establish that marriage was God's gift and help to man. So God's purpose was to provide a companion for man and a suitable helper for him.

Thus, **marriage was not established by God to put us in bondage but to make life easier, beautiful and happier for us. God did not put a burden on anyone**. Marriage is not bondage and it will never be. I am privileged to hear so many youths talk to me about marriage and many of them are seeing this wonderful institution as a burden, bondage and trouble rather than seeing the joy that God intended it for. **Our greatest pain in life can also come from what gives us our greatest joy and pleasure; that depends on how we handle it.** Although the experiences of several people in marriage are not palatable, still that does not remove the fact that marriage was established by God to make our lives better and pleasure filled. Even If the Hollywood, Bollywood, Nollywood, or anyone's experience says otherwise, the purpose of God for marriage was to make our lives happier and joyous. The question then is why are marriages failing? Is it God's fault? Are there things that we are not doing right in marriage? Why should something meant to bless us becomes a source of sorrow to several people all over the world? These and many other issues are what God has laid on my heart to share with you in this book.

CHAPTER II

Why Do You Want To Get Married?

All I could see all over her was desperation and the anxiety to get married now; a beautiful young, talented, gifted and focused lady. I tried to calm her down and explain to her why she needed to wait for God and wait on God but she seems not to be hearing everything I was saying. All she wanted from me was approval for her to go on with the man she has seen; at that point I decided to ask her why she wanted to get married but she could not give me an answer. I looked at her with pity because I know that she is just feeling the unnecessary pressure that so many young people are feeling which is why many of them are rushing into marriage without preparation.

Is marriage all about sexual intercourse and procreation? Sexual intercourse seems to be a major reason that many people are rushing into marriage, but is that the purpose of marriage? Of a truth Paul highlighted that it is better to marry than to burn with lust (1 Corinthians 7:8); nevertheless, so many people are married but are still burning with lust. **A man or woman that chooses to get married because he cannot control his or her sexual desires and cravings will still not be able to control himself even in marriage**. Marriage is not a cure for infidelity and sexual intercourse should not be the reason that anyone will give for getting married. **There are quite a lot of people that are enjoying**

good sexual intercourse in their marriage but are not enjoying their marriage. Marriage is not all about good sex although good sex is an ingredient in marriage. God wants you to enjoy sex in your marriage and that I will explain more.

Is marriage all about child bearing? There are so many marriages that have broken up because they had delay in child bearing or because they are having difficulties in having children. Yes, most of our wedding programmes often states that marriage is made also for procreation and Malachi 2:15 also affirms this but the scripture does not say that that is the sole purpose of marriage. God blessed them and commanded them to be fruitful after he had told them the purpose of marriage; He never told them that it is child bearing that is the purpose of marriage. Permit me to establish here again **that it is possible to have children in marriage and still not have a happy marriage, while there are so many people that are enjoying happiness in their homes despite not having children yet**. It is the desire of God for us to have children and be fruitful in our marriage but that is not the purpose of marriage. Anyone that chooses to get married just to have sex and children is definitely entering marriage with an erroneous view of marriage and a wrong motive.

Why do you want to get married? **You can do the right thing for the wrong reasons and that alone has defiled the purpose of what you are doing**. In the African setting, marrying a wife is just like employing a 'slave' in ancient times. The wife has different assignments such as taking care of the house, giving birth to children and meeting the husband's sexual desires, but is that actually the truth about the essence of marriage? Will God establish the marriage institution just to enslave the woman or put a burden on the man? **No one is fit to marry until he or she has a clear understanding of why he or she should be married**. What happens to the marriage that is built just for sexual satisfaction when the couple's appetite for sex begins to wane as they grow old? Or what happens to the marriage that is built solely for the goal of having children when there is delay in marriage.

Another reason that people chose to get married is societal expectations. The people in this category sees marriage as a societal function that everyone must fulfil. Their view of marriage comes from what the society says, they believe that getting married is fulfilling a requirement to be respectable in the society. Their decisions and principles for marriage is built on what the society says and these kind of people often live a life of pretence. They go about doing all that is in their power to be acceptable in the society, for them, it is all about societal acceptance and applause. They care less about the purpose of God for marriage and in most cases pretend to be happy even when they are in unexplainable pain. My friends, marriage is not about societal acceptance or meeting expectations set by people for you. Your cultural sense of marriage may be in direct violation of the order of the Almighty God that establish marriage, therefore, no one should marry to be accepted by the society. No matter what reason that people give for getting married, until you come to understand why the manufacturer of marriage manufactured the institution, you are not fit to be married.

Check The Manufacturers' Manual

I bought a phone sometimes ago but I did not take time to read the manual of the phone. Few months after I bought the phone, I saw a friend's phone that had the capacity to navigate the road and take him to wherever he wants to go. I was so impressed by that phone that I was already taking the decision to buy the same phone. As I was still admiring the phone, my friend requested that he wants to see my own phone. He then said to me that why am I under using the phone. He then pointed out to me from the manual the various things that the phone can do that his own phone cannot do, including the one that I saw on his phone. I was so ignorant of what I had because I never took time to read the manufacturer's manual. My friend, **no one can explain a product better than his manufacturer and that is why the manufacturer explain the product in the manual that is placed along with the product**. Hence, most people do not bother to read what is in the manual before using the product and that explains why many of us do not maximize fully the potentials of the product.

Many people have attempted to explain what marriage is, using their own experiences, the experiences of other people, the knowledge that they have gathered from various books that they have read, what some people taught them and what the society explains about marriage. Nevertheless, only a few people do consult the manufacturer's manual so as to enjoy fully the marriage package. **You and I must agree with that marriage is solely God's idea and if that is true, then no one can explain marriage than Him**. Hence, He has given us the details that we need to have in His word and that is the authentic source information that is needed to build a lasting marriage. Many of us have read books on marriage and we are already confused, but we have not read the Bible which actually contains the most important information about marriage. Let us briefly explore the word of God and address the issues that we must pay attention to if we must build a godly and a lasting marriage.

Should Everyone Get Married?

What will you say if I ask you this question? Do you really think that everyone should get married? Will I be standing against the counsel of God if I say that not everyone should marry? But that is the bitter truth, the fact that

God established marriage to make our lives better does not mean that everyone should be married.

The most important question...

I believe that one of the problems our generation is having is that we are asking the wrong question and that is why we are getting the wrong answers? So many people are asking, when should I get married? Who should I marry? Where should I marry? What will I wear on my wedding day? But they are not asking the most important question, which is **why does God want me to marry? Why should I be married?** If you do not know the purpose of something, most likely you will abuse it; therefore, **not everyone should marry because not everyone knows why God established marriage neither do they understand the pattern that He ordained for a sweet marriage.**

Oh, I am not talking about Eunuchs here but I sincerely can say that **anyone who does not know why God initiated marriage should not marry**. Do you remember when the Pharisees came to test Jesus on the issue of marriage and divorce? What was His answer? He said 'from the beginning it was not so' Mathew 19:4. What was the Lord trying to do? He was directing them to His intention and purpose for establishing the marriage institution in the first place. **The first prerequisite for getting married is having a right understanding of why God established marriage. Anyone that does not have**

this understanding and chose to get married is the one going into marriage blindly. One common belief about marriage is that since the couple intending to get married do not know each other, therefore they are going into marriage blindly; nevertheless, the truth is that those that goes into marriage blindly are those that have no understanding of why God established the marriage institution.

Genesis 2:18-26. 'And the LORD God said, [It is] not good that the man should be alone; I will make him a help meet for him. And out of the ground the LORD God formed every beast of the field and every fowl of the air; and brought [them] unto Adam to see what he would call them: and whatsoever Adam called every living creature, that [was] the name thereof. And Adam gave names to all cattle, and to the fowl of the air and to every beast of the field; but for Adam there was not found a help meet for him. And the LORD God caused a deep sleep to fall upon Adam, and he slept: and he took one of his ribs, and closed up the flesh instead thereof; And the rib, which the LORD God had taken from man, made he a woman, and brought her unto the man. And Adam said, this [is] now bone of my bones, and flesh of my flesh: she shall be called Woman, because she was taken out of Man. Therefore, shall a man leave his father and his mother, and shall cleave unto his wife: and they shall be one flesh. And they were both naked, the man and his wife, and were not ashamed. (KJV)

Marriage is not about what people think, says or want!

Marriage was not the idea of any man or a group of people, government and the society at large, then it will be wrong for anyone to decide to get married because someone thinks he or she should be married, because his parents or a group of friends and family thinks so or because it is a norm in the society. God in his infinite wisdom instituted marriage after He made man and discovered that man was alone. Yes, He made every other animal with a mate but Adam had none, so God decided to make a woman out of the man that He had already created. He did not force the man to accept the woman as his wife but when the man saw her, he accepted her as the bone of his bone, flesh of his flesh and then went on to name her woman. Therefore, if you are to ready to enjoy marriage, you need to go back to understand why God decided to establish marriage.

Frankly speaking, not everyone should marry. **It is only those who have come to discover the need that God saw in Adam in their own lives that should think of getting married. Why will you bring someone into your life to be part of you when you really don't see the need for it? Why will you ask somebody to join you in your life when you feel satisfied living your life alone? Why make someone get into unnecessary trouble trying to fit into your life when you actually never wanted to share life**

with another person? God saw that it was not good for the man to be alone, so the first question here is, have you seen that vacuum in your life also? If you must even think of getting married, then you must understand what God was saying here. He was not saying that Adam was lonely but that he was alone. Thus, God created a companion for him.

Is it not strange that so many people who are married are still alone? Why? They do not understand that the original intention of God for marriage is to provide us with a companion each, so that we will not be alone in our life's journey. **If you therefore do not see a need for a companion, should you then be married?** You cannot enjoy what I made if you do not understand why I made it and use it for what I made it. **How can you enjoy the institution that God started when you have no idea of why he started it and how He wants it to be run?** No one can explain a product better than the producer. It is quite unfortunate that people are not even interested in studying the manual of God on marriage and they are thinking of getting married. Hope you will pay attention to these issues if you are getting married. You cannot live your own life in marriage; it is either you are ready to live with someone else together as one or, you do not trouble yourself bringing another person into your life. After all, it's your life you want to live.

It is not about age?

The first marriage started when God spoke it to being: The man Adam was not busy with the thoughts of having a wife; it was the Lord that saw the need for it and made him conscious of it. Your marriage plans must be motivated by the instructions of the Lord. One of the major issues I see with so many people aspiring to get married is anxiety and worrying. The society has implanted in people unconsciously that there is a certain age a man or woman should get married, whether the person himself or herself has seen the need for marriage or not.

God created the desire in the man when he said it and the man was not overly anxious. He simply slept and allowed God to make the woman. **Our lives was planned by God not by us, therefore we can simply get nothing good out of life by anxiety but by patiently sticking to the plan God has made for us. He makes all things beautiful in his time says the preacher**! As I travelled around speaking to young people, all I see in youth is anxiety about marriage. So many of them wants to know when they should marry, who they should get married to but do not want to ask the most important question which is why should anyone be married.

It is indeed not good for a man to be alone but the Lord said I will make for him a suitable helper for him, not that the man started struggling to make a woman for himself. You can't make a good woman for yourself, you can't even get a good wife yourself, you need to go back to the one that said it and let him guide you through the process.

Why is it not good for the man to be alone?

Ecclesiastes 4:9-12 *"Two are better than one, because they have a good return for their labour: If either of them falls down, one can help the other up. But pity anyone who falls and has no one to help them up. Also, if two lie down together, they will keep warm. But how can one keep warm alone. Though one may be overpowered, two can defend themselves. A cord of three strands is not quickly broken."* The companionship in marriage is a relationship that God intends to bring greater productivity and fruitfulness in labour. In the infinite wisdom of God, He already knows that the man will come to a season of falling in life but if he is alone, there will be no one to lift him up. Therefore, this marriage relationship that God was talking about is to help each other to stand when the evil day comes and either of the couple is falling away. The companion that God was talking about is such that can help the man to stand in his lowest moment and the moment of crumbling and falling apart. It is important to note that the preacher in Ecclesiastes called our attention to the consequence of being alone, he said "woe unto him who is alone because when he falls he has no one to pick him up" More so, God wanted a companionship that will produce warmth in time of cold because of a truth there will be a time of cold for every man and there is a need for the man to have someone that can keep him warm and vice versa. Again, the consequence of being alone is spelt out clearly that the one who is alone has no one to keep him warm. In addition, the companion that God intended for the man will help the man to be victorious because where his strength will fail, there is a companion for him to fight by his side. Victory is more guaranteed for someone who is married than for someone who is alone. If anyone is alone, he will be easily overpowered. Therefore, God who knows all things said "it is not good for the man to be alone", why then should a man who is limited in all ways claim that he does not need companion.

Note that when God said it that it is not good for the man to be alone, the man became aware that something was missing and not complete about him. He then began to see if he could find among the animals that God brought to him to name because God's word to him already created the awareness. Hence, in Genesis 2:20b, the scripture recorded that, 'But for Adam there was not found a help meet for him.' What does that suggest to you that the process of searching did not begin for Adam until God said it? Our major problem today is that we want to succeed in what God originated without the one that originated it. It is strange that we now live our lives based on what we feel is right and what the society dictates to us, not on the plan that God has mapped out for us before we were born.

CHAPTER III

Excuse Me! Who Do I Marry?

'And the Lord caused a deep sleep to fall upon Adam and he slept...

Genesis 2:21a'

Oh that we can also go to bed like Adam and allow God to make the partners he wants to make for us, the partners that will suit us, fit us and help us in fulfilling destiny. Many people that want to get married have subjected themselves to unnecessary pressure because they have been made to believe that, it is with their human reasoning that they can get a good spouse. **God is the only one that can give a good partner because He made us and made plans for our marriage.** Solomon said in Proverbs that 'houses and lands are inherited from parents but a good wife is a gift from the Lord'. This implies that I need to work hard or earn the favour of my father for me to get houses and lands but that is not enough to get a good wife. Only God can make a good partner and that was why He made Adam to sleep, so that Adam will not make a wrong choice.

One foundational problem with marriages is that the choice of spouses was often made wrongly without consulting the Almighty God. People are making their choice of spouses under pressure, using human yardsticks and by following their natural senses alone. We must not forget that if Adam had called a goat his helper that would have been his helper; so for him to be saved from making an error that will destroy his future, God made him to sleep. Permit me to say that **God needs him to sleep so that he can work things out for him**. Adam cannot be working and God will be working on the same issue; he needs to let go and allow the one that brings the thought of marriage into his heart to help him make the woman that will suit him and fit his destiny. If Adam was awake at the time God was making the woman, he would have been struggling with what God was making because he will not probably understand what God was making and why he was making the woman that way; but it was God that made him so he is the only one that knows what suits him. **If a marriage will enjoy rest, the process of choosing who to marry must begin with a deep sleep, that God can make the partner that will enable the rest in the future.** If the man refuses to sleep, he will make his own choice and definitely at the end he will regret it because only the one that created the man knows the end from the beginning.

The heart of a man is deceitful above all things and desperately, who can know it says Prophet Jeremiah. I have heard so many people saying that I know him or I know her, when in the real sense all you know about the person is the appearance, you really don't know what is in the heart. The great prophet Samuel would have made the greatest error of his ministerial life, if he had allowed the appearance of Eliab to deceive him to anoint him as the king of Israel. It was that day that the great man of GOD learnt that what God is interested in when he makes his choice is not what we can see. Is this not a serious matter to ponder on if you are part of those who feels that they don't need God in making the right choice of who to marry? I have spoken with several people who told me 'I never knew that he was this kind of person'. Do not be deceived my friend, if indeed the heart of a man is deceitful above all things and you will still end up marrying from among men, then you need God in making the right choice.

Has it ever crossed your mind what choice Adam would have made if God did not make him sleep? He initiated the idea that you should not be alone, he made the woman or man that suits you, fits you and that will be your helpmeet; why then should you venture into making the decision on who to marry without consulting him. Our five senses are not enough when it comes to choosing a life partner. How you feel is not the most important factor on who to marry because feelings don't last. I remember that we were taught in a philosophy class that there is a need to always differentiate the appearance from the reality. It is possible for something to look like a chair but is not a chair. **Marriage is not a place for trial and error! You have to be certain that the choice you are making is the one that will help you fulfil your God-given destiny.**

There are people who feel that the choice of a life partner is purely an emotional matter: I refer to those people as emotional or compulsive spenders. An emotional or compulsive spender is someone that buys things not because he needs it or because he earlier has plans to buy it but because the thing appeals to his emotion in the moment. He or she decides to buy it just because he or she likes it. People like that often end up regretting because sooner or later they will discover that they do not really have the need for what was bought. They do not consider the futuristic implications of what they do; they are more concerned about the momentary pleasure and satisfaction. In relationship, these are people that jump from one relationship into another; they don't really have an understanding of what they should be looking for in a spouse, but they are quick to start up a relationship with anyone that they are attracted to. Many of them end up calling it love but it is more of foolishness than love. So if you are getting married, let's talk about your choice? Did you consult God?

Gary Chapman in his book 'Five Love Languages', was more concerned about what happens to love after wedding; but from the little experience that I have been able to see and gather from others, I have come to discover that what many people refer to as love before wedding was not really love but mere attraction, infatuation, and emotional attachment. **The decision on who to marry is not just a decision that anyone should take lightly because it is a decision that affects our destiny here on earth and beyond. This is not a decision that you take based on mere liking and**

attraction. It is a decision that must start with God and be founded on the agape kind of love. This kind of love is the one that can build the home because it is not blind but can see the truth about your partner and is ready to still be one with him or her despite the flaws and imperfection.

The wisest among us humans can be played, swindled and deceived. This is why you need God to direct your steps and lead you to the right person for you. Recently, a friend of mine posted a story of a Christian sister who got married to a brother that she met in church. This is a brother that even the church leadership considered as a dynamic, fervent and God-fearing man. He was actively involved in the affairs of the church, devoted to evangelism, caring and gentle. But all of that was mere acting, his real intention was cruel. He was a Muslim who pretended and played the Christian Brother just to marry the lady. Shortly after they got married, he revealed his true identity and started putting pressure on the lady to deny Jesus and join him in his religion. My friend, don't be deceived, there are many wolves in sheep's clothing. It is pathetic that many at times, the people that falls into this error often neglects danger signs that the Lord might be showing them through people and other things. You can only know what a man or woman chooses to reveal to you but the Almighty God who created us all can show you the deepest part of a man's heart. We live in a world where lies and dishonesty is prevailing, so you need the Spirit of the Almighty God to differentiate between what is vague and original. If you are not sure that God is sincerely leading you to marry someone, don't deceive yourself even if you like the person, **the feelings of likeness will disappear in the face of life's reality.**

Do you know where you are going?

Every one of us in this world is likened to a traveller sent on a mission by a mighty man to a particular destination, at a particular time. The traveller must be sure of where he is going, his mission, and the realization that someone sent him; before choosing who to accompany him. **The mission comes first and it is the understanding of where the traveller is going that determines who the traveller will travel with it.** Anyone that is not going where you are going should be considered as a distraction on your journey says Myles Munroe. **So if you are getting married, you must be sure of where you are going so that you won't be asking someone that is not meant for that mission to join you.**

In a seminar recently, I explained to the youths that the word 'relationship' means two things to me; it connotes **'relation' and 'ship'.** It is the understanding of these two words that determines who we journey with it in life. **Firstly, the word relation means that you have something in common with someone.** It suggests that there is a tie between the two of you. Adam recognised that the woman that was brought to her was carrying his bones and flesh. Whoever you will chose to journey with in life must be someone that has something in common with you and I am not talking of physical likeness and temperamental likeness as the issues to consider. There are several authors who have given several tips on what people should look for in who to marry, but that is not what I intend to do because I really do not want to add to your confusion. **The person that you will invite to join you on your life journey must be related to your God and your master. You cannot be serving the Light and you will chose to be in a relationship with someone that is serving darkness. This is the underlying factor for a godly successful marriage.**

"What concord hath light with darkness?" That was Paul's question to the brethren in his epistles to the Corinthians. Amos the prophet also asked, 'can two walk together except they agree?' This is a basic requirement for a godly home; you must be serving the same God and master with whoever you chose to journey with. So many contemporary Christians believes that it does not really matter if the person they chose to marry is a Christian or not, they believe that all that matters is love. **You can't choose to spend the rest of your life with someone who does not believe in what you believe in and is not interested in serving your God.** Several fine Christian sisters have fallen into this error of marrying a Muslim, but now it is too late for them to get out. Ask them, their lives are filled with tales of sorrow and regret. Stop fooling yourself that religion is not a barrier in love or that you will end up changing the person.

The issue here is clear; **you cannot ask someone that has no allegiance to your God to join you in following your God**.

Above all the popular talks on temperament please pay attention to this. Are you two related in serving God? Abraham knew the weight of that when he told his servant to swear to him that he will only pick a wife for his son among his relative and that he will not go to another strange place to get a wife for his son (Genesis 24:2). You have to be related by God and purpose. **God is the ultimate tie that should determine who you will marry**. God brought her to the man says the scripture. If the daughter of the devil marries the son of God, how will the in laws relate? A believer cannot marry an unbeliever. Your faith should be your major tie. That is what should link you together. If you are sure that, you both are related in God, you can be sure that you can call on your God together in agreement in times of crisis and trials.

Is it a must for me to marry from my church?

Recently, several church denominations began to make rules and principles that forbade young people from marrying outside their church denomination. While some of the churches held on to this rule strictly, some of them just encouraged their youths against marrying from other denominations. A lot of young people have confronted me with questions on what they should do about this. A brother shared with me recently that his pastor is not supporting his choice of life partner and would not even want to be involved because the lady is from another denomination that his church doctrines do not align with. He said that the pastor quoted various scriptures to convince him that he was making a mistake by choosing to marry the lady, since God does not want us to be unequally yoked with unbelievers. He asked me passionately what must be done in that situation.

The tie that I talked about that must prove that you are related to the same God does not mean that you must marry someone from your church. The fundamental issue that must be established is if the person has actually surrendered his or her life to Jesus just like you. It is possible that you attend the same church with someone and the person still does not serve your God. It is not the issue of attending the same denomination that is to be considered as the tie that reveals that you are related with whoever you chose to get married to. Your church denomination does not necessarily make you devoted to God more than others. **What connects us together as Christians is the blood that Jesus shed on the cross of Calvary, so we are to be one family, with one faith and one kingdom**. Do not let any church tradition enslave you; you should marry a child of God, not just your church member. The fact that you attend the same church with me does not make me related with you in faith. There are quite a lot of pretenders in the church, pretending to be worshiping God with you, just to deceive you.

In the church where I grew up as a Christian, there were certain criteria that anyone intending to get married in the church must meet. There is a committee that was set up by the church to decide such matters. Most people ended up having serious problems with the committee because the committee started seeing themselves as the all in all over marital issues; they started deciding who should marry who and who should not marry who, they sat to dissolve several relationships which have great prospects of becoming great marriages. This committee ended sending several youths away from the church because of their high handedness in handling issues. Rules and several regulations were given to people and this caused many more people to run away from the church to other churches to get married.

I know many of you are familiar with this kind of issue and you are asking questions on how to handle such matters. No church is permitted to set any regulation that contradicts the scripture for their members. The church committee is not assigned to choose life partners for people, they are often set up to guide the members and help them resolve issues that look difficult to handle in their relationships. Therefore, when dealing with difficult and unreasonable church marriage committee, you must avoid rebelliousness and be patient in handling matters. Do not get enslaved to any doctrine or rules that cannot be established in the scriptures but be wise and gentle in making your resolve known to the church leadership.

The church marriage committee is not supposed to sit in the place of God in deciding who is fit and not fit to marry each other; even if the marriage committee has sincere reasons why certain people should not be married, they are to guide them with wisdom in this delicate matter. No one will be responsible for whatever choice that anyone makes in marriage except those that made the choice which is why nobody should make that crucial choice for you. **Your marriage is your choice but you should not disregard counsels from God.** You must be able to discern rightly and be sincere with yourself on the counsel that is given to you. It will be foolish for you to run away from a church that is guiding you rightly on the matter of marriage because counsel brings us safety and help us to see things that we might not pay attention to on our own.

What about marrying from my tribe and culture?

One of the challenges that most people face when they are about to get married in Nigeria is convincing their parents of the choice they are making. A lot of parents have superstitious believes about certain cultures, tribes and even communities; this often makes them to instruct their children never to marry from such tribe, culture or community. Should anyone disobey his parent? No! What then is expected of me as a child who is sure that my choice of who to marry is the right choice but my parents are insisting that I cannot? We can never deny the fact that many of our parents have information that we do not have. Many of them are familiar with certain character pattern in people from some cultures, tribes and communities and out of love; they will forbid their children from going to such places to choose a life partner.

I had a friend who could not marry the lady he loved and that he has been in relationship with for years because the parents said no to their daughter getting married to a man from his tribe. Parental blessing is a major factor in marriage but parents ought not to force their decisions on the children. They are expected by God to guide the children in the way of the Lord and all tribes belong to God. **There is no culture, tribe or community that does not have weaknesses, flaws, and errors, evil and bad traditions. So that should not be a yardstick for choosing a life partner. Marrying someone from your tribe, culture or community is not a guarantee that your marriage will work.**

In resolving such conflicts with parents, you must realise that you are not permitted by God to disrespect or dishonour your parents in any way for any reason. Therefore, you have to start by asking God for wisdom to convince your parents about your choice. In as much as the hearts of kings, chiefs and everyone belongs to God, God will definitely give you the needed wisdom to know the right word to say and the right way to say it, that your parents may reason with the decision you have taken. You cannot in any way ignore your parents, rather patiently convince them from God's word that what matters is the connection in Christ and not tribal or cultural connection. In addition, you can speak with your relatives who can also help you speak with your parents. On this matter, a lot of patience and prayer is needed. God is always in control and this concern is not beyond him. Remember that the fact that your parents disagree with you gives you the liberty to disrespect them.

Secondly the word 'ship' illustrates a travelling instrument that is used on the sea. Hence, it is important to note that two people cannot be on the same ship if they are not headed the same direction. **Where you are going determines the ship you join; a man cannot be on the way to Lagos, Nigeria and join a ship travelling to France from South Africa**. Where are you going is the question that matters here? If you are going to France from South Africa and you are already in a ship going to Nigeria, any decision that you take to join the ship going to France makes your journey longer, difficult and painful. It is on where you are going that your heart will be set. **You cannot join yourself**

with someone that is not going where you are going. The person will be a burden to you than a blessing. This is the reason so many couples are just enduring painfully their relationships because they got joined with someone who is not going to where they are going. **Where you are going is what matters. How can you be joined to someone that is on the way to a different direction to where you are heading to?** You won't be able to make progress because as the person is pulling you to his or her way, you too will be pulling the person. You must be sure of your destination when you are choosing who to company with. Is his vision and purpose in line with yours? Is her vision and purpose in line with yours? Until you are sure don't assume that you know.

What about Prophets?

Confusion was written all over her face as she shared her story with me. She said 'pastor I sincerely don't want to make mistake in the choice of my life partner and I have been praying about it. Hence, I met this brother whom I am convinced will be the right choice for me. I decided then to inform my mother about him since you have taught us the proper way to establish a godly relationship. When I told her, she was glad that I did and then she requested that I write for her the full names of the brother. I did and to my amazement, a week later, my mother told me that I cannot marry him and that I should stop having anything to do with him. I pressed her to know why she will say that, but that was when I discovered that she took the name I gave to her to a prophet that she claims is her spiritual father and he was the one that said I should not marry him. Pastor, I am confused because I know in my heart that he is the right person for me. My mother is even threatening that if I refuse to leave him, she would disown me and not bless my marriage. Excuse me sir, what should I do? I do not want to disobey my parents'. Is this story familiar? This is just one out of numerous cases that I have on my hands to resolve. I have recently watched a relationship of eight years break up because of this prophet matter. How do we handle this?

    Let me start by pointing out again that marriage is solely God's idea from the beginning and every marriage that will succeed must be built on his principles. It is true that we live in a time when we are being invaded right and left with strange and false prophets. Yet, **the real preys of these prophets are those who are ignorant.** They are gullible because they do not know God and are not ready to pursue a relationship with him. God started raising prophets when the Israelites told Moses that they cannot come close to God nor approach him because they were afraid of death. Thus, they chose that Moses should be the channel through which they will know the mind of God. Moses therefore had to stay in God's presence to get a message for the Israelites. Take note of the fact that it was not God that said he cannot be speaking to them directly; it was the people that demanded that they will prefer that God speaks to them through someone than speak to them directly. Yes, that was the origin of the prophetic ministry in the Bible.

Does God want to speak directly to his people? Yes, he does. He spoke to Abraham and from that relationship it confirmed that God indeed wants to be friends with us his children. Nevertheless, the office of the prophet remains till today and that is a medium that God can choose to speak to his children. Prophets are servants of GOD that God himself sends message to for his people. But, as wonderful as that is, the real intention of God is to be able to communicate directly with all his children through the Holy Spirit. But just like in the days of old, many of us are so not interested in having a close relationship with God and we chose to approach God through a prophet. **A prophet is not supposed to take the place of GOD in the lives of the people and because God already knows that many false prophets will arise, he decided to place His Spirit in us and give us his word so that we can clearly confirm if what anyone is telling us in the name of the Lord contradicts the nature and character of God.**

Jesus died and the veil of the temple was torn in two, as a symbol that God wants direct access from his children to him. He does not want intermediary but many of his children are not willing to pay the price of having a close relationship with him. **Many people see consulting a**

prophet as a short cut to reaching God and a means to avoiding the time to be spent with God. Nevertheless, the problem with seeking God through a prophet is that the prophets are also human and are prone to human errors. The matter of sentiment often comes into play on certain issues and it is indeed those that seeks the prophets that are at disadvantage because what they are seeking the prophets for, God intends to inform them personally. It is a pity that prophets are now been consulted the way herbalists and demonic mediums are being consulted. God wants to reach his children directly.

It is not biblically right for a man to seek prophets to know who to marry. God sends prophet to his people not that the people go to the prophets to ask who they should marry. Why do I need to meet a prophet on who I should marry when God is willing to tell me directly and personally? **Marriage is a matter of personal conviction and not a family issue.** You should not disrespect your parents but your parents will not be responsible for your marriage. **Even if a prophet tells you what to do, your conviction on the issue is what matters because on the long run, you will be the one to live with the choice that is made and not the prophet.** It is so crucial that you do not ignore prophecies but you should strive to have a cordial relationship with God so that you can say confidently the difference between a prophecy that comes from the Lord, from the human mind or the devil.

The issue of marriage is so delicate that a wrong step taken can ruin a man's destiny. You should not even think of getting married when you are not yet weaned from what your parents say. **The true symbol of maturity lies with your ability to take a decision and stand by it even in the face of opposition**. If your parents are prophets addicted, then you need to prayerfully and patiently help them see the truth that it is your marriage that we are talking about and that the best they can do for you is pray for you. You need not fight them or argue with them but patiently ask the Lord to help them see the truths. It is a shame that most of these prophets will tell you the problem but not the solution.

Many young people are regretting over the choices that they allowed their parents to force them into based on the so called prophetic instructions. **Yes, there are genuine prophets, called by God and whose visions are accurate but they are not to replace the personal relationship that God intends to have with you.** You too should have a witness in your spirit whenever anyone claims to be telling you something in the name of the Lord. **You have to be receptive but sensitive to find out if what the person told you contradicts what God has told you personally before or what is clearly written in the word.** Our laziness in this generation as Christians makes it so difficult for us to devote ourselves to seeking God who has promised us to seek Him while He may be found. God is always committed to guiding his children in the right path they should go.

My friend, if I am close to my father and we see each other daily, do I need a prophet or an intermediary to tell me when he is speaking to me or to approach him for me to know if He is in support of a decision that I am about taking? Why are you running around looking for whom to tell you who to marry as a child of God? Is God indeed your father? What kind of relationship do you have with him that you cannot recognize the voice of your father? Our problem is that the one we claim is our father does not have a relationship with many of us. It is one thing for me to claim that I know someone but it is another for the person to also know me intimately. Jesus said my sheep knows my voice, which means they will never have problem recognising the voice of a thief as different from the voice of their owner, because they are used to him. The LORD promised that when you and I get to the crossroad and we are wondering which way to go, that we will hear a voice behind us, telling us the way to go. That is enough assurance that God wants to always speak to us and guide us but when he speaks, can we hear him or can we discern that he is the one speaking? Is that not why we keep looking for prophets?

Getting married successfully and enjoying the marriage for the rest of your life entails that you make the right choice but making the right choice does not lie with your parents or any prophet, it lies with you. I do not intend to turn you against your parents or your pastors, but I am calling you to understand that marital decisions are decisions that involve only three people, your spouse, God and you. Marriage is not for children as I have said earlier, it is for those who are matured, who are weaned from societal dictates, parental dictates and pressure from anyone. Marriage is for those who are matured enough to have a personal conviction on issues of life, who will be willing to stand for what they believe in and will allow no situation, pressure, and condition to dissuade them or persuade them otherwise.

God could have just imposed Eve on Adam or instructed him immediately after making her that he must marry Eve but He allowed Adam to see her as the bone of his bone and the flesh of his flesh. Eve was made for Adam but he needs to be convinced himself that she is the bone of his bone and the flesh of his flesh; which will eventually lead him to call him the right name. **Your personal conviction must be your own personal discoveries as you relate with your maker, it should not come from an outside source like from prophets, parents and friends.** It should be your personal conviction although God can use others to confirm to you what He is saying to you.

What about Compatibility?

This word compatibility has been used wrongly and out of context severally by people in relationships. I know someone who broke up a relationship of seven years because he concluded that he is not compatible with the lady. It makes me wonder what compatibility really is. Does compatibility have to do with you and your partner behaving the same way? Does it mean that you and your lover should have the same temperament? What is the yardstick that we should use to measure compatibility? A lot of people believe that they have to marry someone like them because God made Eve to be like Adam. To be like someone does not really mean that you are a perfect match with the person. We must know that God will never make a mistake because he will never put a round peg in a square hole and vice versa.

Moreover, **God does not lead us in making a choice that will only benefit us for the moment; He is more concerned about our future**. Many of the people making marital choice often do so considering only the temporal issues about the person they intend to marry; they consider physical appearance, present status and other irrelevant issues. Compatibility to some people is when a dark person ends up with someone who is also dark in complexion or when an outspoken person is in a relationship with someone who is also outspoken. Compatible in English is synonymous to the words well-matched, like minded, well-suited, similar in temperament and companionable; hence the real issue is how do we define that we are well-matched, well-suited and companionable with another person? Having similar temperament is considered as a yardstick by many authors on marriage as a factor that determines compatibility and this has led so many people astray.

Nevertheless, **the wisdom of God is often not the same as the wisdom of men**. Men want people of the same character traits and temperaments to be husbands and wife but most of the time the wisdom of God attracts people of opposite temperaments to each other. God is always perfect in His ways and that was what He showed when He made Eve for Adam. **God will not just give us what we want but will give us what we need to fulfil our destinies and live a glorious life**. Most times we think that we know exactly what we want out of a woman or a man but we are limited as humans to just what we see now and that is why the wisdom is in allowing the one that knows the end from the beginning to lead us in choosing what is best for us. **What is best for us may not fall into our yardstick of compatibility as humans**. Our definition of compatibility is mostly limited because what we know about each other is so limited. The scriptures made it clear that the heart of a man is deceitful above all things and desperately wicked, who can know it. Indeed, the only word that is close in meaning to compatible among other synonyms that I mentioned above is to be like minded with another person but to know the true state of any one's mind, we truly need the wisdom of God and his help to discern the right from the wrong.

Some have based compatibility on just educational status and societal status, while some just left it as temperamental similarities but to God it is deeper than that; because what the Lord wants for you is a partner that is a suitable helper to your destiny. **He or she has to be someone that suits you, that fit you and that has all the help you need to be able to live a fulfilled life.** He or she does not have to be of a similar background, status and temperaments with you to be that. God took the bone out of Adam to make someone for him that has the capacity to be his friend and a helper that will also fill his void and strengthen him in his weakness.

I have seen God attracting two people who seems to have opposite features but not opposite mind-set. The mind-set and the heart of who you are going to marry must be right with yours. God often brings a hawk to marry a turtle, so that the two of them can have what is lacking in each other and be complete. The hawk will ordinarily fit in marriage another hawk but God often brings a turtle to a hawk; that should explain why most times a quiet person ends up with a lousy person. The hawk flies and the turtle walks, but God who does not make mistakes knows that the hawk needs a turtle so that he can learn that there will be time when he should not fly and the turtle needs the hawk so that the turtle can also learn to fly when the need comes for it. To humans it is a mistake but to the all-knowing God it is never a mistake because **God will not give you what you already have, He will give you what you lack. If God gives you someone that possesses the same strengths**

and weaknesses that you possess then you definitely do not have the suitable helper that you need. This is the crux of compatibility; it is not about you having the same physical features with another person or emotional similarity, societal fitness and to be matched educationally. It is when you and the person fit into each other's life by bringing what is lacking and needed to each other.

It is essential that we always remember that **what fits you may not fit me**. You may desire to have something that I have but you must remember that our uniqueness shows that God has designed for us all to have what fits us not just what people wants for us. Adam needed an Eve that was created by God to fits him and enable him to be complete. Eve's configuration by God was for Adam; she was taken out of him and made for him to be a suitable helpmeet for him. I want to emphasize that this is the wisdom of God to give unto us all who fits us not just physically but someone who is made of God with the abilities and the capacity to be our helpmeets. If you wear my shoe, no matter how much you try to manage it or adjust it to fit you, it will not, because it is my shoe, made for me and it only fits me well. If I run with someone else's shoe, I might not be able to run fast as I should because I may not be comfortable in it. It may even harm me wearing another person's shoes because they are not meant for me. I can do anything to make the shoes fit me but the difference will always be there; this should help you understand why so many people are just enduring their marriages and are not enjoying it.

If you must have a glorious marriage, in your choice making, you must put this at the back of your mind that you must be able to measure the compatibility of the person you want to marry by her qualities and capacity rather than by mere appearance and temperaments. You must know her strength and be able to relate with her weakness. He or she is given by God to be strength to you where you are weak, thereby suiting you completely and enables you to live a meaningful life. Adam saw Eve as the bone of his bone and the flesh of his flesh, meaning that he saw himself in her and saw what is lacking but is needed in him in her. Compatibility is a very crucial matter if you are getting married but not in the way many people are handling it. **Your compatibility starts and ends with having the same mind, seeing the same vision even if you see it in different ways, believing in the same God and goals, even if you see the process differently and standing for the same thing**. Disagreement on likes and dislikes does not necessarily show incompatibility. You both will like things differently and view things differently because you were not raised in the same way, which is why you will have to learn what it takes to relate with someone different from you before you rush into marriage. It will be foolish for you to expect someone that is just getting to know you to be like you and it will be more foolish for you to use his or her not been like you as a yardstick to measure your compatibility for marriage. You should pursue to discover if that person has the basic things that you lack and needed to enable you live life and is able to enable you enjoy true companionship.

Divine timing...

So you have decided to get married? But you must have read the scriptures that there is time for everything. **The matter of divine timing is another factor in preparation for marriage because wisdom is doing the right thing, in the right way, for the right purpose, with the right people, in the right place and at the right time.** All of the points that are mentioned in the definition of wisdom above must not be ignored. You have to marry the right person in the right way, for the right purpose at the right time. No matter what you do, when it is done at the wrong time it becomes wrong. You must be sure that your planning for marriage fits into God's perfect plan and agenda for your life. Many of the people that are going into marriage are rushing into it out of pressure. A man once told me that **anything that is done in haste is never done well**. We have a lot of fast food restaurants but they lead into more trouble for the person that consumes it because the food is not often well cooked. You should not rush into marriage; you must be sure that you are going into it at the right time.

God often uses the experiences of our lives to mature us and make us grow to become who we ought to be. You need to be sure that you are made before you bring someone else into your life.

Why the anxiety? Why the rush? Why the impatience? I made several mistakes in this area and that is why I am particularly emphasizing it. I use my experiences in most of my writings because I can only be a source of comfort to you where I have been comforted. I was in a hurry like many young people reading this book. I was anxious and desperate because I allowed my background to keep pushing me to look for a way of escape. I have heard several stories of pastors who have failed marriages and I have also been a part of a failed marriage, so the fear of not wanting to fall into the same error kept pushing me to wanting to quickly fix my marital life. I was so much in hurry and that was borne out of fear. I don't know why you are in a hurry, but you must realise that **you can't fix anything in a hurry, else you will always have to come back to re-fix it later**.

On the 1st of April in the year 2001, when the Lord saw how desperate I was about having a successful marriage which was leading me to search desperately for a life partner; it was around 1 am in the morning when the Lord spoke to me that he makes all things beautiful in its time and that I should allow him to handle things at the right time. I didn't listen, so I jumped from one lady to another but the mercy of the Lord helped me. After all my efforts in finding the right lady, I still had to return to the Lord's earliest instruction on waiting. By December 2007, I had had six different relationships and I was tired because none of them was leading me to where I wanted rather they were draining me and making me lose credibility. I remember that as I lay on my bed that night, I cried unto God that I was tired of these broken relationships and he told me to recollect what he told me back then in 2001, April 1st.

I repented of my impatience and then decided to seek God. I decided to wait on God and wait for God. My friend, it is easy to wait on God but difficult to wait for him because within the period of waiting, many of us jump out looking for our will. No wonder God caused a deep sleep to fall on Adam. I had to wait for God and stop running around aimlessly. I remember sharing this story with a young lady recently who was so desperate about having a relationship and the more she tried to help herself, the more she got herself injured. She tried to speak for God before God will even speak for her. Waiting for God is worth it my friend, although it is extremely difficult. I remembered spending that period of waiting in prayer and full concentration on my ministry. It was difficult because I was already used to seeking for my own wife but this time I was not even thinking about it again. On the 14th of February, 2008, as I was meditating on the word of God in my quiet time; I heard the Lord said 'you will meet your wife today'. How and where I do not know, neither do I need to bother myself. By evening of that day, I had even forgotten what the Lord said, but the one that said had not forgotten. My wife followed her friend to a programme in a friend's church where my spiritual children also compelled me to take them to. I never had the plan to be in the church and I was looking so casual for that programme but I went any way.

As the programme ended, my friend's wife asked me when I was going to introduce my wife to the family. I smiled and told her soon; but as I was still chatting with her, I saw my wife from afar and then I heard the same voice that spoke to me in the morning that 'that is your wife'. I did not utter a single word to her or even meet her after the program but today we are married happily. I did nothing to meet her than to follow God's leading, I did nothing to get her than telling her what God told me, I did nothing to retain her than always asking God for wisdom and I did nothing to marry her rather than loving her the way God showed me. You have to learn what it means to wait for God. **Don't learn by destructive experiences. Remember that marriage is completely God's idea and without him you can't succeed.**

What about Love?

A few months after my wife and I began our courtship; I discovered that she was not really excited about our relationship; she was not reciprocating the love that I was showing to her. I got fed up of her attitudes towards me that I called her best friend to ask her why her friend was behaving to me in such manner. She still did not change her attitude, rather she was getting worse. It was obvious that I was the one forcing her to have the relationship with me, so I concluded that she does not love me and that it was best for me to leave her. But before I did that I called her one night and asked her a very simple and sincere question, I asked her if she loves me. To my amazement, without mincing words, she told me no. She reminded me that she earlier told me that I am not her dream man but she decided to say yes to me because God said so. She made it clear that she just liked me and that she does not really love me as I do love her. I got so angry with her response that night but I did not allow my anger to overshadow my sense of reasoning. I sat down to ask myself why she was so blunt and why she has chosen to waste my time in a relationship that she was not excited about. So I decided to call her the following day to find out from her if we should just quietly break up since she has told me she does not love me. She laughed and asked me if I can teach her what love is and how to love me. She told me that she was ready to obey God but she believes that she needs time to learn to love me. All of this got me more worried and confused, so I decided to seek more to know what love is and what loving someone entails.

Was she wrong to have a dream man? No. God has given us his wisdom so it is wise for anyone intending to get married to have a desire on what who to marry should be and the qualities that he or she should possess. But a salient point that she made was that she has decided to submit her own dreams for what God has ordained for her. That explains to me that in the first place, it is possible for someone to be guided by God to marry someone that you do not love at first. She never said she was not willing to love me, she simply said she does not love me at that time but she liked the way I often talked to her. It certainly means that she has something that she liked in me even though she does not love me as I expected from her. It was this understanding that led me to my first personal definition of love. I defined **love as a process of accepting someone unconditionally without expectations.**

My definition of love may not support the popular view of so many people on what love is because love to so many people is sex or emotional feelings that grows between a man and a woman. I was sure then that if it was just sexual desires that I had towards my fiancée then, it was just a matter of time before it would be quenched because the lady in question would not even allow any closeness that would bring about such act. More so, if it was just emotional attachment or feelings, it would vanish since it was not being reciprocated but love for me was greater than that. I discovered that I had to take a decision to be her friend, accept her and stay committed to making her happy whether she returns such gestures or not. It was not easy to do but I also had discovered that she is the one that I should spend my life with.

If you are getting married, you must remember that you either live for momentary pleasure in your relationship or make greater sacrifices to have a glorious marital future. **Love is not all about satisfying your sexual desires or about romantic involvements or feelings in a relationship, it is all about what you are willing to give up to ensure that you enjoy marital bliss in the future.** Most of the young people in relationships today do not understand this definition of love; they only understand the language of sex and romantic feelings. The height of love to so many of them is sexual intercourse, buying of gifts and visiting eateries and beautiful places. **Love transcends the very use of beautiful words; it is wired and built around sacrifice and selflessness for any marriage that will be sweet and beautiful.**

This understanding got deeper as I read books and paid attention to several issues in our relationship. My wife who was my fiancée then particularly told me that she had a weakness in that she loves to be independent. Yes, that might sound simple but that was a major challenge because she can't be independent in a relationship. I do have the option of trying to change her, accept her or let her go. What choice do you think I made? It was a very rough way of learning what love is. It was then I discovered that **the real opposite of the word love is selfishness. You can't be**

selfish and love, in fact those that truly loves must have died to self. Love is not infatuation or mere liking. You can't meet someone today and just love the person immediately; yes, you can be attracted to the person instantly but to love takes time. I hope that explains to you why it is popularly said that the true test of love is time? **The love that grows into a beautiful marriage grows over time, it is not a magic**.

Fools fall in love?

I know that you are familiar with the phrase 'fall in love'. **Falling in love suggests that the relationship just happened as a result of a magic wand of love that suddenly happens to someone**. No one plans to fall, so it removes the sense in the preparation for the relationship. You can meet someone that you like suddenly but that should not be confused for love. Falling in love is what I explain as a mistake that someone was not prepared for and because it just happened, in a matter of time when the reality of what is involved begins to dawn on the person claiming to have fallen in love, the person deliberately wants to jump out. It is not impossible that an attraction to someone can lead to a glorious marriage. Of a truth most of our relationships starts with attraction and revelation. The problem is that many people conclude on the level of mere attraction, they don't press further for revelation. We should not forget that the devil can use beautiful things to lure us and trap us and that is why it is not all that we are attracted to that we get attached to. Between attraction and attachment comes revelation and reasoning. To people that believes that choosing a life partner is just a matter of attraction and likeness; they always throw away the need to seek God and to sit down and count the cost before making commitments.

A comic movie that I watched as I grew up was titled 'Why do fools fall in love?', reveals the error of young ladies who got attracted to a talented singer who was also rich but never paid attention to the details about his life. At death, all of them were shocked at the amazing discoveries of who they fell in love with; because they were foolish. I know you have heard people say 'love is blind', the truth is that love is never blind, it is lust, attraction and infatuation that makes people go blind because it is always filled with excitement and emotional displays that lack reasoning and planning. **Love is a decision to commit yourself to making another person a priority in your own life and that kind of decision is not just taken by mere excitements and wishful thinking.** You love with your heart, soul and spirit not with just your body. Mere feelings lead to stupid decisions, so don't expect to take this great decision of whom to marry on mere feelings. Be sure the love is pure and agape.

Our courtship was filled with many misunderstandings but it was also filled with discoveries. We both discovered love. She didn't love me at first but she grew to love me and truly love the real me. There are times that God will lead you to discover that someone that does not fit into your dream plan is your spouse and you struggle with accepting that; I want you to know that if you submit to the will of God; you will learn to grow to love the person. **Loving someone is not a frivolous matter; it is a crucial matter that should not be handled with levity.** I must emphasize again here that children should not marry because **the decision to love someone comes with risks but also with the willingness to stick to the choice of the person that you love at all times**. Such willingness, readiness and sense of responsibility only come with maturity. Most people that walk into the church for holy matrimony do not know this nor have they grown to that point when they can hold on to the decision that they have taken to love someone for the rest of their lives. **So if you must get married and enjoy it, be sure that you are truly in love with the person, not that you are just emotionally attached to the person.**

One major word that I used in my first definition of love is acceptance. I am one of the few that enjoyed so much sincerity from my fiancée. She opened up to me on some of her flaws but there were several issues that she didn't mention, nevertheless, the onus is on me to accept her with her flaws. My eyes will never be blind to those flaws but I must accept her, and then see how I can help her with the flaws. Was I perfect? No, I was not and I am not now;

but she had also learnt to see my terrible weaknesses and flaws and still hold on to me. That is what defines love. Have you heard the reasons people give for breaking up their marital relationships or for divorcing their spouses? It is disheartening that for them, love ends when what they see in their spouse is the opposite of what they are expecting.

CHAPTER IV

Now That You Are Married!

It's time to say good bye...

I was scheduled to be interviewed on a Television channel recently; the topic to discuss was why some ladies still prefer to bear their fathers' names in marriage when they ought to have changed completely to their husbands' names. Some of the people that were present at the pep talk felt that most of these ladies are not confident of the status of their husband so they prefer to retain the identity of their powerful or rich parents. Some of them felt it is ladies from very rich and influential families that are involved such. Why am I telling you this? **Many of the people that get married are not actually prepared to leave where they are coming from.** It is a very serious issue confronting marriages in our generation. Many of the people that are getting married do not want to abandon the lives they used to live, they do not want to part way with where they are coming from, so they want to live their own life in the new life they have chosen to start.

Marriage is not joining together of two different worlds but the abandoning of two different worlds to start a new one was one of Norman Wright's definitions about marriage. What is most common nowadays is that people carry where they are coming from into their marriage, expecting to live a new life. So many wives are carrying their parents' home into their new home, while so many husbands' expects the wives to be what they have seen of their mothers. My friend, **if you must get married and be successful in it, then you must be ready to forget where you are coming from and start your own world with your own spouse**. **Every marriage is unique and you can't expect the experiences that you see in other marriages to be your own experience**. You cannot bring the bed that your parents lay into your husbands' house as a wife; rather you and your husband will have to lay your own bed, so that you will not always have baggage's and burdens of the past as a source of conflict in your home. So are you ready to say goodbye?

'For this cause shall a man leave his father and mother and cleave to his wife', was the declaration of the author and initiator of marriage. **The starting point of a successful companionship is the willingness of the couple to abandon where they are coming from completely with the understanding that they are now in a new world and they have to accept that decision as a better world.** There cannot be merging of where you are coming from and where you are now, you have to choose where you belong to and work on making it beautiful. If you are not ready for this, then don't marry. You will no longer need your parents to interfere in your home, your friends don't really matter and your society holds no ground in your marriage; what matters is you and your spouse. If you are not ready for that reality, then don't just rush to the altar.

As simple as these issues are, they are fundamental to the success of any marriage. We can no longer continue to allow people take this most important decision of life without thorough education of what it entails. I have seen enough tears and heartaches, which I don't want to see more due to failed marriage. I would rather prefer you taking your time for marriage than rush into it and fail. God does not want you to fail in your marriage; He wants you to enjoy it. He wants your home to be a heaven on earth but that can only happen when you build it on His pattern and principles. If He said, you must leave your father and mother to cleave to your spouse, then you must be ready to leave. There is no debate about this. **Men and women over the years have tried to change God's order and principle of marriage but have failed woefully**. He is the originator, he alone knows the formula that can work, so no one can succeed outside the principles he has outlined in his word.

God did not make any mistake in making the best for Adam. He made a suitable helper for him but Adam will never be able to unlock this treasure if he does not take the step of abandoning everything that he used to know before the woman, so as to establish a beautiful relationship with the woman. If you must get married and enjoy the beauty of marriage, you need to be willing to lay aside these encumbrances. **You have to make up your mind either to**

be married to your spouse or to where you are coming from, your parents or who you used to be. Remember that there is no merging. You have to leave without looking back. No matter what happens on your way, you have to be ready to keep going with the person you have chosen to go with. Before you say yes I do, be sure you are ready to do everything that is required of you.

"I do" means "I do" to everything. As simple as that statement is, you must realise that it is a vow that you made both before God and His people. It is not a statement that you should make without thorough consideration and preparation. Once you said you do, you must be ready to leave everything behind you. You must be ready to leave anyone that you think matters in the past and make your spouse the only one that matters. Without leaving, cleaving will never be possible and becoming one will be impossible. The ultimate desire of God is your becoming one with your spouse but that is a product of several processes. **Before you say I do, please be sure you will leave and leave for good.** There are people who keep making reference to who they used to be, where they used to be, the status they had attained before, the calibre of people that they used to relate with and what they used to have; but as long as that all of those is not erased in their hearts they will find it difficult to allow the owner of that place to stay there. **It is not compulsory to get married, so don't put yourself under a burden. You don't need to ask someone to be**

part of your life, if you are not willing to let that person into your heart and be part of it completely. If you are so attached to your parent, you better stay with them and forget about marriage. You need to leave.

I do not intend to scare you away from getting married. Marriage is a beautiful estate; a lot of people are enjoying their marriages, one of whom I am. I sincerely want you to be married and enjoy your own marriage too which is why I am taking the pain and time to prepare you for the reality in marriage.

Break free

Your marriage should not join the list of other failed marriages. Pay attention to the issues raised in this chapter. If you must get married, stay married and enjoy marriage, you need to realize that you have to prepare yourself first. **Marriage is not a magic that just happens, it is a process and you have to prepare yourself for the realities involved. So many of the people that have issues in their marriage now, failed to prepare for the journey they were embarking into.** They were not thoroughly informed about what the marriage life is all about. They did not spend time to find out from the initiator of marriage what his intentions, purpose and plan for marriage is. Is that not why we have so many marital abuses and perversion today? How can you write an examination and expect to pass when you know nothing about the examination? Prepare yourself before starting this journey. **Marriage is an empty cup, it is what you bring into it that you will find in it and that is why you must prepare yourself well so that you can bring the best into your marriage.** Don't let your choice be based on what others think, stick to God and be sure that you are taking the right step. So you are getting married?

Lastly as I round off this chapter, I would like to call you to remember that you attract to yourself what you think about and what you focus on. What was our experience in our first year of marriage? I may not have the right words to describe it but all I can simply say is that we fought almost every day until there was nothing to argue or shout about. But one night after we had argued, we both got tired and asked ourselves why we were always fighting. That night, we both discovered one of the truths that will eventually help our home become a place of sweet love. Recently we looked back and laughed at ourselves because we now have that understanding that is needed for us to live as one. I know you are curious to know it, so let's talk about it. **Do you know that all of us are products of various things combined together? First we are a product of our backgrounds, which is simply what we have seen, experienced and heard as we were growing up. Secondly, we are a product of people's experience around us**

and unconsciously this also shaped us to what we are now. Thirdly, we are a product of what we learnt both at school and various religious institutions and lastly we are a product of our environment. All of these that I have mentioned has unconsciously formed our perceptions about life and I have come to discover that many marriages are broken today because they have not freed themselves from the negative perceptions and opinions that they have unconsciously built about marriage.

I grew up from a broken home and I really do not know what a good home was but I also learnt from books that I read that many great minsters of God were destroyed by their wives, so unconsciously I saw every woman as evil. I remembered that whenever we had a quarrel, the first thing I would say was, 'I have already been told that you, my wife, are the devil that will ruin my ministry.' What was I reacting to? What I have heard and read about minister's wives. I was never seeing my wife as a gift from God but from the wrong perceptions and opinion that I have as I grew up. When you ask some men, they will tell you that when you marry a beautiful wife, she will never submit to you. Do you know that such ideas are from our backgrounds? **If a man stays too long in the dark, he will think that everywhere is dark.** Many ladies who have heard several evil stories about men, who have seen several men maltreat their wives, and who have seen some particular movies and read some particular novels may conclude that all men are mean and wicked. But does that mean there are no sweet and loving men? If we do not avoid such generalizations, they will soon become our expectations and then become our experience. **If the only picture of a wife that you have is evil, then you will never see anything good in any woman, even if your wife is the best.** So my wife and I discovered that we had actually built wrong perceptions about each other and that was why we were defending from becoming the victims we had imagined we might end up being. We lived that one year in fear. We never trusted ourselves; we both were just looking for an opportunity to validate our opinions.

Do you know that many people don't want to marry because they are afraid that what they have heard and seen in other homes might happen to them? Many of them that even got married have conclusions made about their spouse's, so they can never see anything good in them. Why can't we rid ourselves of this loads that are standing on our way of experiencing joy in our lives**? If you must marry and enjoy your home, then you must abandon where you are coming from, lay aside all those opinions and just trust each other to build your own world.** If you don't break yourself free from your background, you may end up experiencing the same things you saw and hated in your background? **Break free please, don't let the experience of others ruin your own life**. I am not saying that you shouldn't be careful but don't allow that to make your marriage another sad story. Even if you had been abused, you can deal with it and move on to enjoy a blissful home. Thank God my wife did not end up becoming what I feared and I never became what she feared. **If they told you that everyone failed in marriage, why not ask them about those who succeeded?** You should not fail, change your perceptions and you will be surprised at how wonderful your spouse can be. Change it now, remember Job said, 'what I feared has happened to me'.

Our minds are like magnets that have the capacity to attract the contents of our thoughts to us and that is why many people have already failed in marriage even before they stepped into it. Let your mind set about marriage be positive and be more focussed on success and not failure. I have emphasised in this chapter that God wants you to enjoy your marriage and it is that desire of God that should constantly motivate you and make you to have confidence as you approach marriage. Don't let your mind be occupied with fear, let your mind be rest assured that even if everyone around you fail in marriage, you will not. No matter what you have seen, heard or experienced in the past about marriage; let it not pollute your mind about marriage because I know your story will not be among the stories of those that failed. Have confidence in God and prepare yourself for a blissful marriage. Now that you are married, leave everything and cleave to your spouse.

CHAPTER V

This Bride And Her Groom...

The vows are exchanged, the young man has just said 'yes I do' to everything that was said, so also the beautifully adorned damsel with all smiles has just said yes to pledge her life to the man she loved. I paid close attention to the words of their vow and I heard them say 'I take thee as my lawfully wedded wife (husband) to love and to care, to keep and to protect, in health and in sickness, in poverty and abundance, in all situation until death do us part'. Then there goes the priest, as he blessed them and calling forth the various witnesses to attest to the vows that the new couple has made by signing the marriage register, which is followed by the great declaration that everyone has been waiting for: 'I now declare you husband and wife'. The priest then went on to say to the jubilant crowd that what God has joined together, no man should put asunder and they all said amen. Hence, the question that strikes me at the moment is that, have they truly become husband and wife? If they have become husband and wife, is it the ceremony that made them husband and wife? Or is the certificate or the vows that they have exchanged before the people? Why should they in the first place been given a certificate when they have not gone to any school? Yes, they had several sessions of counselling with the priest but does that mean that they have been thoroughly prepared for marriage. Now the wedding is over and the marriage is about to begin and they have certified them as husband and wife. What exactly determines that these people have actually gotten what it takes to be married? These and many questions filled my heart as I sit quietly in the crowded auditorium

It was a few minutes after ten in the morning, on that beautiful Saturday morning; the minister had just declared them husband and wife and everyone can obviously see the joy written all over the newest couple in town. The couple had extended this invitation to me, to be part of their wedding celebration and to be the guest speaker at the occasion. It was a wonderful time that we have had in that service all along and the choir had done their best in giving us very beautiful musical renditions. All eyes were on me as they waited to hear me exhort this new couple within a few minutes; I was dressed in this fitted suit, waiting for the choir to finish rendering their piece so that I can declare the mind of God to the expecting crowd. All of us in that auditorium were conscious of time and that means I could only speak for a few minutes.

The time came and I was invited to the pulpit to speak. As I stood behind the pulpit, the Holy Spirit spoke to me and said tell this new couple that they are not yet husband and wife. I was so shocked to hear that, so I went on to tell them what I was instructed to tell them. The countenance of most people in the church changed instantly; you could see that they were shocked to hear that from me. I made it clear to them what the Lord told me and after a few minutes;

the couple were all smiles applauding me for sharing what the Lord laid on my heart to share with them. Let me share briefly with you the content of the message.

Have you ever asked why the new wedded lady is not called wife on her wedding day but bride and why the man does not bear the name husband at that instant, but groom? You may be wondering why I am playing around with those words, but I have come to discover that **it is the bride that becomes the wife and it is when the groom has succeeded in his task that he is called husband.** What do all of these imply for those who are getting married or have gotten married? **The wedding day is actually the day the marriage journey begins and most time, people expect the new couple to become husband and wife instantly**. I have wondered for a long while, why the new couple that has not yet passed through any phase of the marital life will be first issued a certificate.

The Proverbs 24:3-4's COUNSEL

The writer of Proverbs 24:3-4 actually let out a secret that is crucial for any marriage that will be blissful and that will not collapse. He revealed that **marriage is in three major phases**, namely the building phase, the establishing phase and the beautifying phase. Many of those who are married only stop at the first phase and then begin to complain that their marriage is not working. It is just like when someone intends to collect the Visa to travel to another country, he must first apply for the visa and pay the visa fee, scheduled an appointment if necessary or submit the required documents for the visa to be processed and then pick it up. You cannot apply for visa and pay the fees and stop at that point, you must be willing to do the other things required to get the visa. **The first phase of marriage is what so many people are mostly concerned about; that is the phase they prepared for and that they spend heavily on.** A lot of work goes into this phase because we have been deceived to believe that that is the only thing that marriage is all about.

The building phase requires wisdom according to the writer of Proverbs. Why does it require wisdom? Simply because it involves doing the right thing, at the right time, in the right way, with the right person, in the right way and for the right purpose; and for that to be achieved you need divine wisdom and not just earthly wisdom. That is the phase that required searching for the right person to marry, laying the right foundation for the relationship, discovering and designing the plan for the marriage, planning for the ceremony and getting the right people involved and other fundamental things. Simply call that phase the getting married phase and that is what the first part of this book seeks to address. The wisdom that is needed for this phase is what the first part of the book has been assigned to help the readers discover.

Hence no marriage can succeed by just staying at that level; the couple has to be ready to move on to the next phase which is **the establishing phase**. The establishing phase is a phase that the writer of Proverbs said requires understanding. **It means that the couple in marriage must move on from the wisdom to get married and be ready to understand what it takes to establish the union.** This phase is what I called the phase to **stay married**. If you look at the world of marriage, you will agree with me **that it is not every one that gets married that stays married**. In fact, it is so pathetic that the number of marriages that collapse each year is alarming.

It is not as if most of these marriages were not built well but they were not established. The problem is that only few people understand this principle that you need to pursue understanding to ensure that your marriage is established. **It is what is well established that will stand firm and last.** The reality of your marriage facing the wind, the storm and the flood are there but when your marriage goes beyond the level of just being built to being established, then you can have confidence that it will not crash no matter what happens. I believe that the Lord will help you as you read to possess the understanding needed to establish your marriage. The third phase of marriage as described by the writer of Proverbs will be considered in the other chapters of this book. **I am sure that you now understand that your marriage cannot succeed at just the stage of getting married?**

The truth

It is true that no one goes to school to learn marriage and since our lives are formed by the various experiences that we have in life, and then we can agree that **our background or the home we grow from is our first school where we learn anything about marriage.** The danger of this is that not many of us had the opportunity of seeing what a good marriage really is, so we grew up with distorted information about marriage. Some may actually escape this because they were privileged to have been raised in a beautiful home and where they see a great exciting example of marriage but I speak for the majority who had to learn by asking painful questions. I once heard of a young man who grew up seeing his father always beating the mother and concluded that that is the best way to show love to a woman. In addition, the schools that we attended are part of our real marital training because there we learnt so much from the experience of people that we meet in our schools.

The church is another place where we ought to be prepared for marriage because **marriage is seen as a pattern that Christ Jesus showed in the way he loves the church and gave himself for it**. In fact, the church is considered as the bride of Christ. The media also serves as another source of information that has formed the ideal of several people about marriage; what is seen on the television and what we hear on the radio seems to go a long way in informing us about marriage. Lastly the experience of people that surrounds us either destroys our confidence in the marital institution or encourages us. Frankly speaking **many of us have not been privileged to see a good marriage and we have not had the opportunity of learning the right thing about marriage.**

How are we expected to perform such a miracle that just few minutes after we have been joined together in holy matrimony, we can suddenly become husband and wife? All along we have spent time and energy preparing for this day but I really don't think we have prepared ourselves for the life after wedding is the untold heart cry of so many people getting married. Nevertheless, the truth that you must face as you begin this journey is that **your wedding is just a means to an end and not an end in itself. The certificate that you have been given is to certify that you have started your marital journey and not that you have completed anything.** All those that attested on the certificate are there to stand as witnesses to the reality that you have fulfilled what is required to live as husband and wife. The title husband and wife is your identity in the society but you have to be ready to make sacrifices and work hard to truly become husband and wife.

Marriage is not a magic that happens immediately after wedding, it is a process of building over a period time which calls for wisdom and hard work. The wedding ceremony is just the foundation laying ceremony and it is only a fool that will start rejoicing that the foundation of his house is laid and will abandon every other thing that needs to be done. The foundation laying process is indeed a very serious task and one should be happy to have successfully laid the foundation. At this juncture, let me emphasize again as I have taken time to state in the previous chapters that everything about marriage must be founded in God. In as much as I will be talking about the other processes involved in building a glorious marriage, we must not forget that **a faulty foundation will in turn destroy everything that is built in the future.** This is the reason that you must pay attention to laying a solid foundation built on God by his wisdom and garnished by knowledge as you step into marriage. Jesus spoke of a foolish man who built his house on the sand and a wise man who built his house on the rock, but when the wind, flood and storm came it was how the foundation was built that determined which of the houses that remained.

The foundation laying process starts with you alone, your spouse and God. When you have succeeded in laying this foundation, you then involve your parents, your church and the public to come and witness what you are intending to build. The pastor in agreement with your parents then gives you the approval that they are sure of your capacity to build and they are happy that you are intending to build your own home. Yes, it is custom for us to celebrate with you and laud your bold, courageous and wise decision to build for yourself a glorious home **but from that moment that**

everyone have returned to their own homes, you have to start building and continue building until you can be happy in your homes. No marriage started as a complete building or as a finished project and that is why I laugh when I meet guys or ladies who claim to be looking for a readymade wife. So you have work to do to ensure that you build what will give you joy and sooth you.

Jesus as the master builder recommended that anyone that intends to build will have to sit down first and count the cost, so that he will not end up with an abandoned project or an unfinished building. I remember that in my village, there were a lot of abandoned buildings that were never completed. When you get to these buildings, you can see for yourself that resources and energy has been invested into such buildings but they were never completed and all of that often end up as a waste. Several reasons were given by some of the owners that I met and some of the stories that I heard confirmed that many of the owners of such buildings had died without completing them. Some of my friends believe that most of these owners faced spiritual attacks and that was why many of them did not finish the buildings while others believed that many of the owners were not able to complete those buildings because they could not gather the resources to finish. No matter the case, we have so many uncompleted buildings just like we have so many abandoned marriages and Jesus our Lord in his great wisdom counsels everyone intending to build to sit down first and count the cost. **If so many people in marriage actually sat down to count the cost before starting to build, they may never have to abandon their marriages**. Yes, the devil hates marriages but our lack of preparation has also led to the ruins of many marriages which are what the previous chapter is calling your attention.

In this chapter, I will liken marriage to building like I have started doing and I will also liken marriage to going to war and other things that will explain the points that I believe that the Lord wants us to emphasize in this book. Should we stop after we have finished laying the foundation and we have thrown a great party? Should we just sit down waiting for the blocks to fall on each other and be arranged by automatically? Is it wise for us to just expect things to happen in our marriage just because we have had a great wedding? This is the problem that many marriages faced after wedding that make them crash quickly. After the wedding, many couple just sit down and start relaxing, expecting the marriage to work, expecting a miracle to happen and expecting the flame of love to keep burning. That is mere day dreaming my friends.

Marriage is not just a dream. When you wake up from the dreams you need to back it up with necessary actions. You can't just assume that the flame of love that has been kindled in your relationship will just keep burning. **No lamp**

keeps burning forever without regular addition of oil and maintenance of the lamp. You have to be ready to add more oil after the lamp has been lightened. You have to be ready to mould blocks, buy more sand, buy cement, get labourers and continue building if your house will be completed. You are the one that determines what becomes of the building and no one should be made to pay for your incompetence and laziness. Let me remind you of the following:

It is your home that you are building

Do not be deceived to think that people will build your home for you. **You should not even expect your parents to be involved in the building of your marriage; they have their own marriage to build and to continue to build.** No matter how intimate you are to your parents, you have to leave them and cleave to your own partner so that you can build your own home. This is the ultimate reason that marriage is not for babies who are still attached to the umbilical cords of the parents. It is for those who are matured, those who have already been weaned and not those who will sit down waiting for an outsider to come and continue the building that he or she has started. You and your husband or wife must have drawn the plan together in courtship and the marriage time is the time to execute it. It is not the time to expect your church, friends, pastors or prophets, siblings, family and the society to build a plan that you drew.

The greatest error lies in spouses expecting that it is their partner that should build, while doing nothing. It is your marriage and the two of you are responsible for whatever happen to that building. We all witnessed the foundation laying ceremony and we are sure that you will not call us to see what you are doing if you are not determined to do it. **Marriage is not about what your partner will do in building, it is what the two of you will do together in building your home.** One of the major weaknesses that we all inherited from Adam is passing of blames to each other, which will not allow our homes to last if we don't watch it. In counselling with most people who are intending to be married, I always point it out to them that marriage is an empty cup and it is what you bring into it that you will find it.

If you have the opportunity to hear many of the couples that come up for divorce, you will discover that one major issue with many of them is that they failed to accept responsibility for their marriage. Many of them are often busy shifting the responsibility for their home to one another. **You can blame anyone that you want to but the truth remains that it is your marriage and not another's. If you refuse to mould the blocks, your marriage will definitely remain the way you left it. It is your choice and you must remember that**

whatever you do, it is still you that will be affected either positively or negatively. The best anyone can do for you is counsel you or pray with you but the ball lies in your court, how you play it will not affect the person that counselled you. You have to pay attention to this truth so that you will not allow anyone to lead you to abandon your marriage because even if you chose to abandon your marriage because you feel that your spouse is irresponsible, you will still have to stick with someone else and rebuild again; but in essence you will still fail in the same place of accepting responsibility for your home. **Do you think that by abandoning this building that you have started because you feel your spouse is not responsible, you will find it easy with another person that you choose to build with again? The grass may look green at the other side; you will discover it is not necessarily so. Stop thinking that you have options because it is a fool that start building and refused to complete but jumps to another site to build and when he is tired of that one, he will still go to another place to build.** How many uncompleted buildings do you want to have, when you could have patiently waited to build one successfully?

It is your marriage, so **from the moment you are declared husband and wife, get to work**. Start building according to the plan that you have drawn in your courtship. You have shown the world on your wedding day that you want to build, why don't you just get to work instead of looking for who to blame for your failures. I remember my father in law told me when I was about to get married that I should not expect anyone to build my home for me and that I should never come back to him to report my wife to him. I thank God that counsel helped me to realize on time that it is my marriage and that it is left for me to be take responsibility for home.

One of the major problems that face building of godly homes is the issue of external influences and interference from parents and sometimes friends. This issue has led many homes to their abrupt end because they refuse to treat their home with the sanctity it deserves. No one should have the right to interfere in the building of your home except God. **Your marriage should be built on that understanding and you have to be ready to accept responsibility for whatever becomes of your home.** In conclusion, remember that failure begins when you neglect your duties and expect others to take responsibility for you. You should not expect your building to just be completed when all you have done is to lay the foundation; you must take the necessary step to complete the building after the foundation is laid. No marriage is just successful; it takes commitment and hard work.

CHAPTER VI
It Is Time To Be The Groom And The Husband....

The concept of being the husband in many parts of the world and many culture is very faulty. While so many men see themselves as lords of their homes, there are those who sees being called husband a title or empowerment to be boss in the home. Hence, only few people do have the understanding of the purpose of God for men as husbands. The man is vested with so much responsibility that if we have the understanding of the gravity of these assignments, we will be better men. Firstly, it is important that we pay attention to the fact that God sees husband as the head of the wife, just as God is the head of the man or Christ is the head of the church. Therefore, the man has been called to an esteem place of leadership and sacrifice. Secondly, when you look at the head of the body, there are definite functions that the head performs that determines what happens with the other part of the body, which is to see, to listen, to think, to speak, to perceive or smell. Thus, the man has the task to hear God for his family, see things ahead or have a clear vision for his family, listen to the other parts of the body when there is a suggestion or complaints, speak with or speak to the family, perceive things when they are wrong and to provide a sense of direction for the body which I refer to here as the family. In view of this, the purpose of a man transcends the folly of lording ourselves over our spouses or merely being the boss.

Why is the newly wedded man called groom and the bride called bride? Why is it that the foundation of a building does not equal to the building? A friend of mine got tired of his wife barely just six months after the big wedding ceremony. He complained bitterly to me about her and told me that he has concluded to break up with her. As he was talking with me, I began to sense in my spirit that another abandoned building project is in the process and that we must find a way to stop it, so that their marriage will not join the list of marriage casualties. My friend complained bitterly to me about her and told me that he has concluded to break up with her; he went on to say that he was sure that he made a mistake. My friend is just like so many people out there who are contemplating to break their marriage because they are feeling disappointed in whom they got married to. **Many of them felt that their expectations were not really met and the only thing they must do is let go of the lady or the man.**

I did not respond immediately to what my friend said because I knew that I must tell him the right thing, so I went home and asked the Lord what to say and that is what birth this message. Many men have broken up with their wives because they end up not being the wife that they have dreamt of. But they have forgotten that on their wedding day was when the man was commissioned for the new task. They won't call the woman wife on her wedding day but bride, because it is the man that will groom his bride to become the wife. That is why the man is called 'groom'.

What does it mean to groom?

The word groom means to clean up, tidy up, prepare, trim, brush up and spruce. If we pay attention to the meaning of this word, then it will help us as men to realise that our duty as the groom is not just a matter to joke with. To groom is to clean something or someone up which explains that the lady in question has not come into your house as a saint or a clean person and the first duty of the man is to "clean her up in Christ" and ensure that whatever is not supposed to be in her is removed. Also, the groom is expected to tidy up and prepare something or someone for the purpose she is to serve. This innocent lady that has just joined you on your journey really needs to be prepared for the task of been a wife and that task is not something that anyone can prepare her for without your involvement. **She needs to be tidied up, trimmed, brushed up and spruced so that she can be the wife that God intends her to be**. God made her the weaker vessel and it is the man who is the stronger party that is to help her fit in the role of a wife. The task of grooming takes patience and time, which is not something that anyone should just rush into. In the first chapter, I emphasised the need for preparation before taking the decision to get married because the commitment of a groom is not for boys who cannot stand on their own decisions. It is not for children who are been tossed around by all manner of counsels and advise; it is for those who are patient enough to accept the tasks and responsibilities involved in marriage.

Grooming has to do with patiently nurturing, teaching, tending and helping someone to become what he or she should be. It is therefore believed that a man that takes a woman to the altar of marriage is matured enough to patiently groom his bride to become the wife. The man is not supposed to just expect the bride to automatically become the wife, she must be groomed. Hence, **many of us men built unnecessary expectations when we were getting married, we want a magic to happen to our wives, we want them to become what we have had in mind about who we want our wives to be; not considering the fact that the woman does not know what is on your mind except you teach her**. It does not really make sense that a man is expecting his wife to be what he has always dreamt of without helping the woman to know what the dream is and then help her gently to fix into the dream. We build expectations that are not often realistic and when they are not met, we pass the blame to our wives.

Our expectations are often too unrealistic, because we don't remember that change takes time and we can only expect something from someone that knows what

we want. As a new pastor of a village church, I wanted to implement changes quickly and that made me to constantly encounter opposition but when an elderly man of God explained to me that anything that is done in a hurry is never done well. He made me realised that change takes time and within that time, a lot of hard work, patience and endurance is needed. **Why do we make the mistake of even attempting to change our wives instead of accepting them first, teaching them and then patiently help them to become what we want them to be**. So before you think of breaking up, have you groomed her?

Time has been referred to as the true test of love in any relationship, which is why we must allow patience to be a virtue that we men must possess. A man is required to love his wife just like Christ love the church and gave himself for her, so that she can be a prepared bride fit for the heavenly wedding. The assignment given to us as men towards our wives is such a heavy one that requires so much sacrifice and giving. **We cannot perform our duty of been a groom if we cannot love our brides the way Christ loves the church.** The kind of love that is needed for us to be able to successfully discharge our responsibility as a Groom is the Jesus' kind of love, the love that accepted us while we were yet sinners, the love that gave itself for everyone, the love that does not expect and a sacrificial love. **If every man can love his bride the way Christ loved the church and groom her to be the wife that she ought to be; most marriages will**

not crumble. The reason it is difficult to patiently groom our brides as men to become wives is that most men do not possess the kind of sincere and true love that Christ has for us. In a generation that defines love as emotional feelings, marriage will surely crumble because that is not the kind of love that can make marriage successful.

Many people have asked why so many men find it difficult to love their spouses the way they loved them before marriage. Although several reasons have been given by many preachers, counsellors and authors as why the love shown before marriage is not the same as the love shown in marriage by men; nevertheless, the truth remains that most men do not really possess the kind of love that is required of a man that can succeed as a husband and build a godly home. **Selfishness for me has been the only opposite of love and it takes a selfless man to truly be a groom and then be considered as a successful husband**. You have to understand that Christ's love is the standard for marital love to be expressed by a man. Christ loved us even while we were yet sinners, which means **we are to love our wives even with their weaknesses and help them to become what they ought to become**. Christ Jesus did not love us because of our good qualities, so we are not permitted to just love our wives because of their good qualities. Christ Jesus also loved us by giving himself to us; therefore, we must be ready as men to give ourselves to our brides, if we will fulfil our responsibilities as grooms. To give ourselves simply means that we must not just be ready to give gifts to our brides but giving ourselves is the ultimate gift that is expected of us if we must succeed in building a godly home. **Any man that will succeed as a groom must possess the Jesus Kind of love.**

Most men do not really give their brides the opportunity to learn, the time and patient to be made into the wife that they desire to see before they eventually give up on them, describing them as misfits. **Jesus never gave up on any of us and that is why we have been enjoying his mercy and grace; what right do we have then to give up on our brides**. Our problem is that we are so selfish that all we are concerned about is what we will gain from our brides on the immediate, but we must see beyond what we want and help our brides to become the best that God desires them to be. Before you think of breaking up with her, have you given her time to understand you? Hope you realise that a turtle will never become a hawk? As I mentioned previously, God often brings people that are opposites of each other together in marriage so that they can help each other in their place of weaknesses. **If your wife is weak where you are weak, then how will you complement one another and how will you get the strength that that you need from each other? The problem with many of us is that we don't accept people before attempting to change them.**

Of course, our wives are not from our backgrounds, so it will take time for them to adjust. We must stop trying to change them, accept them, love them, teach them and be patient with them; that is what grooming is all about. She is going to be your wife but she is your bride now, so groom her. **On your wedding day, you were commissioned to build your home and one of the major pillars that you must build so strongly is the grooming of your bride. She is one of the pillars that will make your home last; therefore, you must patiently groom her.** Stop complaining about her, she may be a turtle and you a hawk; she cannot fly so be patient with her. I don't believe that your marriage can't work, be patient and allow God to help you.

What does it mean to be the husband?

'Likewise you husband, dwell with your wives with understanding, giving honour to the wife, as to the weaker vessel, and as being heirs together of grace of life, that your prayers may not be hindered. 1 Peter 3:7'

Another name that the man is called in marriage is husband and I believe that the advance duty of the groom is to be the husband. I believe **that grooming is the foundational level of the man's responsibility in marriage because when grooming ends, the man is still expected to be the husband.** What does it mean to be the husband? Does this word have anything to do with the word husbandry in agriculture? Husbandry in agriculture has to do with growing crops, gardening and farming. Historically I may not ascertain where the name husband came from but **it is not a title but a job description**. The man will never come to a point when he will say that he has done all he can do on his wife, just like a farmer will never stop growing crops if he will harvest bountifully. The day the farmer stops gardening, growing crops and watching over his farm is the day he stops reaping from the farm. **Even after a man has groomed his bride and she has grown to become a wife, the man must still continue to walk with her, work on her and attend to her, so that she can bring forth the fruits needed for a beautiful family**.

Peter in the above text calls on the men to be husbands who dwell with their wives with understanding. What understanding is he talking about? **First, that she is your wife. Secondly, that she is a weaker vessel. Thirdly, that she deserves attention all through her life. Fourthly, that she will never grow beyond the level of the husband's investment. Fifth, that she is your glory and whatever becomes of her reflects directly who the man is. Sixth, the man must possess the understanding that Jesus has been preparing his bride for long by his sacrificial death and constant love, care and blessings towards his church, the bride; and this is what the Lord expects from the man. Also, that the woman is to be treated with honour and as a fellow heir of the grace. Lastly, the man must**

have the understanding that how a man treats his wife determines whether God will answer his prayers or not.

A few months ago, I visited my father in the ministry in his office with my wife. We spent time talking about the ministry but when we were about to leave his office, he looked at me keenly and told me to take care of my wife. I could see warmth, seriousness and urgency in what he said and I kept thinking about what he said to me for several days. **My friends, how a man treats his wife is a reflection of his relationship with GOD and that also will determine how God will treat the man.** God in his benevolent mercy and grace gave you the woman not because you asked for her but because he wants you to enjoy your life and he wants you to fulfil destiny and you must not treat his gift anyhow. So many men have killed their wives, brutalise them and in turn have treated God with contempt. Many of them have called the women that God gave them witches and have ascribed their life's failure to their wives but if you see how they have treated their wives, then you will know why they have failed. God's hears and eye will be shut to any man who does not groom his wife well and grow her as a good husband. **Our assignment as men requires that we learn from Jesus and that we pay attention to the lifestyle of Christ who himself is called love so that we can adequately love our wives and live with them the way Christ lived with us.**

CHAPTER VII

Are You Ready To Be The Wife?

I carried out a research recently and I discovered that so **many ladies who have chosen not to marry are afraid of being enslaved by men.** Their perception is that men dominate the women and once a lady is married, her freedom is taken from her; many of these ladies believe that there is no need to stay in marriage once they can get a child or two out of a relationship with a man. This explains why many of them want to retain their parents' name in their marriage; these ladies are craving for freedom at all cost. A lot of reasons are given for this menace, such as abuse from men and the old African cultural idea of enslaving women. Nevertheless, this error is being passed to the next generation and it is becoming so rampant that many of these young ladies are declaring independence in marriage. I have heard so many of them say 'I will never allow a man to run my life for me'. There are those who want to live their own lives in their marriage, they really don't care about what happens to the marriage, all they want is to have their way on all issues. They have built for themselves a wall of defence and all they are interested in is standing their ground against their husband's directive. Some of these women claimed to belong to the women liberation movement but when you look at their lives, it is often filled with sorrow. **Of a truth many men have maltreated and mistreated their spouses but that does not mean that a**

lady should go into marriage with a rebellious mind, a defensive mechanism, an independent mind set and an arrogant attitude.

One of the key issues that God himself emphasised in the scripture when it comes to marriage is the issue of submission from the wives. **The struggle for control between husbands and wives have led many marriages to a disastrous end**. Thus, the question remains why a woman will join herself to a man that she does not trust to drive them to a glorious destiny? Is it possible for two people to drive the same car at the same time? Will they ever have reached their destination? **It is indeed pathetic that many couples in marriage do not understand the order of God for marriage, neither do they know the roles, purpose and assignment given to each of them before marriage**. God did not make a mistake in His order. The man is to be the head, (the driver), the woman is to be the companion and helper on that journey. While there is so much that is expected of the man, the woman must submit to the man, if they will ever fulfil destiny or enjoy their marital relationship.

The woman is not to be redundant and not allowed to be involved in what goes on in the relationship, the opinion of both the man and the woman is crucial but the woman is commanded by the Lord to submit to her husband. I cannot thank God enough for my wife because I have escaped many car accidents because she was there calling my attention to things that I did not see on the road each time we travelled. We both would be dead by now, if she does not call my attention to the dangers on the road. In spite of this, she does not struggle to take the wheel from me. **There is only one wheel and there can be only one driver, but there are times the driver cannot see what is around or ahead, the helper is there to keep him company, guide him and ensure that they reach their destination safely. A woman is not to be the driver even if the man cannot see clearly. She is to be his help meet. That is the order of God.**

It is impossible for us to over emphasize that there is a need for us to understand what God's purpose and principle for marriage is before anyone steps into it because our world is fast redefining marriage and its principles. God did not make a woman to be a slave to the man nor did he create a woman to be a subject of a man; the woman was made to be a helpmeet to the man and that was why God commanded that the man should love her but the woman also must play her part which is to submit to the man. **The woman is not in a competition with the man, she is not to be his rival but a helper.**

I have noticed that several women became frustrated and angry because their husbands do not listen to them and these has brought their family into grave danger from time to time. **A man that truly loves his wife will learn to listen to her, value her opinion and allow her to be part of everything that is going on in the marriage but even if the man does not have this understanding, God did not command the**

woman to declare her independence from her husband. The woman is not supposed to live a different life in marriage; she was made to be one with her husband. God's purpose of a woman must be clearly understood for a woman to enjoy marriage and I will love to discuss them briefly.

God made the woman out of the man for the man

God has never made a mistake and it was solely his decision to make a companion for the man. In His own wisdom he decided to put the man to sleep and then took the rib from the man to make the woman. **The woman was not made outside the man; she was definitely made from the man, to be able to fit into the man. The first and major purpose of a woman is to be the man's companion, to fit into him. The man was not made for the woman, it was the woman that was made for the man; any other definition is an error.** No matter what anyone defines a woman, it is only what God calls her that is true because he made her. God made man in his own image but made the woman in the image of the man. He used what was taken out of the man to make the woman and that should explain that **no woman can find true fulfilment outside the man that she was made for.** It is unfortunate that so many people are redefining the purpose of a woman; they are trying to make the woman what God did not make her. It was clear from God's intention at creation that the woman was made to fit into the man's life as a companion and to complete him.

It was not even God that gave Eve the name woman, it was Adam. "Adam said: this is the bone of my bone, the flesh of my flesh, she shall be called woman because she was taken out of the man 'Genesis 2:22. **Any woman that will succeed in marriage must remember that her purpose is found in her man; that is the order of God which no man can change.** The first woman Eve was created by God to be a suitable helpmeet for Adam so that he will not be alone. There is no other purpose that God gave the woman. The woman was made to be the helper like the man, God used what he placed in the man to make her so that she will always realise that she has no life outside the man and that the man and her are to be one always.

She was made to fulfil the need of the man

Did God not know that the woman has her own needs? God knows and he has a great plan of meeting the need which is for the woman to fulfil her purpose by fulfilling her husband's needs, thereby fulfilling her own needs. **The woman was made as an answer to the question in the man's life and it is when the woman fulfils that duty that she can also find true satisfaction in life.** Most women who continue to say that they do not need to be with any man or get married before they can be fulfilled in life are merely deceiving themselves, because the main purpose of a woman is not to give birth to children or to make money. **Most ladies are only thinking about their needs when they are getting married and that is why they are not finding true happiness in their marriage.** They do not understand that it is when they fulfil their husband's needs that they can find true happiness and joy in life. God did not in any way intend to enslave a woman, which was why he instructed the men to take the major task of loving the women the way He loves the church. The fulfilment of the man is the joy of the woman.

Paul's explanation

"But I want you to know that the head of every man is Christ, the head of woman is man and the head of Christ is God. Every man praying or prophesying, having his head covered, dishonours the head. But every woman who prays or prophesies with her head uncovered dishonours her head, for that is one and the

same as if her head were shaved. For if a woman is not covered, let her also be shorn or shaved, let her be covered. For a man indeed ought not to cover his head, since he is the image and glory of God; but the woman is the glory of the man. For man is not from woman but woman from man, nor was man created for the woman but the woman for the man. For this reason, the woman ought to have a symbol of authority on her head because of the angels. Nevertheless, neither is man independent of woman nor woman independent of the man in the Lord. For as the woman was from the man even so is the man also is through the woman; but all things are from God. 1Corinthinans 11:3-12"

The above passage has caused controversies among so many Christians because of its application; while some think that the passage is focussed on covering of heads during prayer, others do not believe that that is the issue that is been addressed in the passage. Hence, we must pay attention to the truth that Paul is raising here which has to do with orderliness and order in the body of Christ which is what made him to use the analogy of God's order on His relationship with us and with our spouses. Paul used this analogy to explain the truth about how a man is to see the woman and how a woman is to see the man. Paul did not attempt to belittle women or call them insignificant but rather, he tried to emphasize the order of God that man was made for God, just as woman was made for the man.

Thus, explaining that just as **the man is the glory of God, the woman is the glory of the man**. This implies that **any woman that is not fulfilling her purpose in the man's life has no glory**. Paul took his time to write this to balance the culture of the Jews which has no regard for women. In as much as a woman was made for the man, the man must not be independent of the woman. **God expects that man treats his wife the way He treats the man with love and that the woman must respond the way a man is to respond to God**. The man must not dishonour God in any way and so also the woman must not dishonour the man.

Civilization and Modernization seems to be luring our generation away from God's standard and pattern; but it has led us to more pain than joy. We cannot change the order of God and hope to enjoy his blessings. No woman is made to live independently of her husband. She has no personal life but the life that God has called the man to live. **God did not give the woman a different task apart from the task He gave to Adam.** The man had an assignment which he cannot do outside his wife because the wife is to be his helpmeet. It is unfortunate that this order is been changed daily by people. **Most women want to be married but they don't want to be wives**. They want to be independent in marriage because they have accepted this demonic theory that a man will enslave them. There are so many ladies that have made up their minds from the first day they got married never to submit to their husbands because they have been deceived to believe that the man will take them for granted. Nevertheless, if the assignment given to the man on the day of the wedding is to groom the bride to become a wife, how will he fulfil that duty if the woman bride has already made up her mind not to submit to the man?

"Submit to him", that is the most important task that God has given to any woman if you will be able to build a godly home and enjoy it. The devil wants women to declare independence from their husbands so that they will not enjoy a blissful marriage. My friend, God is so perfect in his dealings with us that he knows that the need of any woman is attention and the need of any man is respect which is why he commanded that the woman submits to the man so that she can receive the attention as he grooms her and that the man loves her so that he can groom her the way Christ loves the church. How can you say no to that and enjoy marriage? I have come to notice that most ladies in marriage exhibit stubbornness and rigidity in their relationship with their spouse and such ladies end up with stories of woes in their marriages.

Should a lady not have a say in the home? Yes, she should. My wife and I constantly had issues on this in our early years of marriage. She believed that I was not allowing her to express herself and I believe that she was not willing to submit to my leadership. We ended up arguing and quarrelling over irrelevant issues because the two of us were not ready to understand the principle of God on marriage. She couldn't trust me because she has always been scared of a man taking her for granted. Even when I was telling her things that will benefit her and help her, she was still resisting because she has her mind filled with the thoughts of a man enslaving her. **It is difficult for ladies to submit when they do not feel secured but they cannot be secured when they do not submit to the man who is to groom them in love. Submission does not suggest that a lady has lost her voice but that she believes in the new leader of her life.**

The illustration of marriage is that of a ship that is set for a destination. The two people involved are both coming from different backgrounds, hence the lady has decided to entrust her life to a man that she believes is to lead them to their destination. She has to leave everything behind her and follow the man to wherever the man is leading them to, without struggles but with love and understanding between the two of them. This is the reason that this decision on getting married to a man is not to be taken lightly. **Before any lady choose to join her life with a man and journey with him on his ship, she must have considered it thoroughly and prayerfully and must have decided to trust the man without fears of accidents.** The woman cannot be resisting the man's leadership and expect no accident on the road. She has to trust him, believe him and support him not disobey him. **If you are not willing to**

allow him drive your life, then you should not go ahead to marry him in the first place, because there cannot be two drivers in your ship. One has to drive, the other has to support. The two of you cannot be driving to different destinations and expects to be at peace. The woman is to recognise that the man has been vested with the authority and responsibility to lead them both to where they are going, so she must submit to the man and support him.

The error that is being spread all around is that women should not trust their husbands to lead their family the way they want, that women should also have a destination in mind and not just sit down as wives being enslaved. Yes, a man is to be the leader with the support of his wife but she must realise that she does not have a separate life from the man. A woman is not expected to be the man, she is to be the companion and the helpmeet of the man; so many women are caught up in power tussle in their homes which is not supposed to be. **The husband and the wife have to be heading in the same direction, living for the same purpose, pursue the same vision and have common goals.** The woman is not expected to be on her own in her marriage. It is indeed true that many men are not leading their homes in the right direction but the woman must help the man in all humility, she is not to make the man feel incapable. **All men react to the feeling of incompetency and that must be noted by the women.** The man and the woman are not expected to share the same view about issues all the time; they definitely will have opposing views and ideas on issues but they cannot have different visions and purpose. If a woman is not willing to submit herself to a man, then she is not ready to fulfil her purpose in life and not ready to be married.

Practical issues:

I heard a story of a Christian woman who decided to give a gift of a car to a pastor but was turned down by the pastor. The pastor held on to the fact that her husband must be in support of such move and that until her husband is in agreement with the gift, he will not take the gift from her. Should a woman keep a separate account from the husband? Should the woman spend her money on her own even if she works? What is the stand of the Bible on this issue? The pastor has indeed offered a great help to the woman and has taught her the true principle of marriage. No matter what the lady has, once she is married, they are not her own. No matter who a lady is, once she gets married she becomes the wife of that man. No woman in marriage should keep a different account apart from her husband except that is what the two of them have agreed on.

However, **the husband also should not keep a different account apart from the woman except if that is what they both agreed upon? Personally, I believe so. While the woman does so out of respect, the man does the same out of love. A woman is to submit everything she is, she was and she intends to be to her man**. She cannot just do things that her husband has no knowledge of. Her husband is the head and the head cannot be detached from the body and the body will still be alive. It is pathetic that so many homes are severed. **A woman cannot be the part of a body and decides to function alone; neither will the man function alone.** The leadership responsibility of the body lies with the head and the other part of the body is to support the head so that the body can achieve his goals.

The pastor was right to reject the gift because if he takes the car, he will be party to destroying the marriage completely. **It is possible that the woman suggests the idea to the husband, but the husband must be in agreement before such gift is given**. God will not break this order. We cannot continue to give excuses for doing the wrong thing. **God did not make a woman to compete with the man or to assume the role of the man but as a helpmeet for the man and when that role is redefined, there will definitely be crisis in such marital relationship.**

Sarah called Abraham Lord!

'Likewise you wives, be submissive to your own husbands, that even if some do not obey the word, they without a word, may be won by the conduct of their wives, when they consider your chaste conduct accompanied by fear. Do not let your beauty be that outward adorning, of arranging the hair, of wearing gold or of putting on fine apparel; but let it be the

hidden person of the heart, with the incorruptible ornament of a gentle and quiet spirit, which is very precious in the sight of God. For in this manner, in former times the holy women who trusted in God also adorned themselves, being submissive to their own husbands, as Sarah obeyed Abraham, calling him Lord, whose daughter you are if you do good and are not afraid with any terror.1 Peter3:1-6'

Submission is not just a call for contemporary women but a secret that has helped successful wives of old to achieve marital success. Peter who is the author of the above passage calls the women to the realisation that it is their submissive conduct that will guarantee their success in their marriages; he explains that even if a woman is married to an unbelieving man which we may see as a wrong choice in our society today, her conduct is sufficient to help the man becomes a child of God. A woman that will succeed as wife must not just pay attention on the frivolous things that women pay attention to in our days. She must not concentrate her efforts on her outward appearance; she needs to work more on having a gentle character, a quiet spirit and a submissive overall attitude. A great wife will seek to fulfil her God given purpose not what the society teaches her to be. The society pays so much attention to how a woman looks and that is what so many ladies are concerned about, but they do not build the character needed to succeed in life. **A woman can make up her face to appear beautiful to her**

husband and people outside, yet she will not be able to make up her character to win her husband's heart and enjoy him to the fullest. In a generation that is concerned about appearance, the reality of marriage is neglected and that is why many homes have the form of happiness but in the real sense, they are filled with sorrow and pain. I see many couples wearing uniforms but are indeed enemies in their homes. Women who truly want to have a godly home and want to succeed in building homes that will last must see beyond what is worn outside but must be ready to do her best in building up the character that is needed for her home.

Women of old may not have had enough time in adorning themselves with costly ornaments but many of them have the testimonies of a successful marital life. **What is the value of outward beauty when the heart is filled with pain, sorrow and regrets?** Sarah is an example of such women who cared not about how foolish people will see her but choose to obey her husband, submit to him and even call him Lord. The success of Sarah was not just in calling her husband Lord but in regarding him in such manner. Sarah would have become a thorn in the flesh of Abraham because of the various 'irrational' decisions that the man was taken but she never left him or fought him for it. Was it easy for her to just wake up one morning and leave her relatives, friends, wealth and the known for the unknown that Abraham claimed that God has commanded them to seek? Was she not foolish to have accepted to follow Abraham to a place that he himself does not know? How easy was it for her to have accepted that Abraham had truly encountered God and that God has commanded him to abandon everything and move to a land he will show them? Did she find it easy to start living in tents and sojourning in strange lands when they have mansions where they are coming from? What a woman? She exhibited the real value of a bride and that is why history has her as a perfect example of one of the greatest wives that ever lived. How will she have agreed to following Abraham in his so called foolish quest, if not that she has trusted in his leadership and have submitted to him in all situation. How many women can follow their husbands in such manner? That is the hallmark of submission that we can see in any woman.

Sarah did not just follow her husband on that foolish trip but was always ready to stand by him, for him and with him at all times. She didn't say no to her husband's request that she should disguise as his sister to save him from death when the sojourn in Amalek and Egypt. **It was a ridiculous request but she counted the value of her husband's life more important than the shame she would bear.** What a woman? She could have chosen not to be part of the plot, knowing well that it will have grave consequences; she could have considered what will become of her in the eye of all people and turned down the request. But she did not forget that she had made a vow to submit her all to Mr Abraham. She knows that her life is in Mr Abraham and the only joy she can ever have is to see Mr Abraham succeed in his mission. She does not have a different plan, she never had an exit strategy, and she honoured her husband daily and was willing to do anything for him to succeed.

As a child I used to think that Abraham was cruel to have listened to Sarah's request to send Haggai and Ishmael away, until I discovered that **it is impossible for a man not to listen to such a submissive woman.** When you hear women complain about their husbands not listening to them, you can also infer that such women are not doing their duties of submitting to their husbands the way they should. I must submit here that a woman that learns to submit to her husband will in turn enjoy the man's attention in all things. Indeed that was the kind of woman that Sarah was. **She never stood against the direction that her husband was showing them, she trusted him and followed him**. I really don't know if it is civilization and education that is turning women against their husbands. What an error? Sarah did not just agree with Abraham even when her pride was at stake, she was also willing to entertain strangers that Abraham brought to the house. **She trusted her husband's judgement in all things and was never seen rebelling against him**. I know that Mr Abraham pushed her when he told her that God has commanded him to go and sacrifice their only son; although the Bible was silent about what happened in the family at that period but we know that Abraham went to the mountain the following morning. Mr Abraham could not have forced his way on his wife, which suggests again that Sarah simply said yes Lord to her husband on the matter. What I can draw out in conclusion was the fact that Sarah obeyed Abraham just like Abraham obeyed the Lord. This chain shows that a woman's submission to the man is also in direct proportion to the man's submission to the Lord; nevertheless, the woman has the duty of submitting to her husband.

Rebecca came down from her Horse (Genesis 24:64)

Another woman who is regarded as a great wife in the scripture is Rebecca. From the first day that she was brought to her husband Isaac, she was great. Yes, she came from a family that is wealthy and that was why the father could afford her the luxury of riding on his horse to her husband's house. This woman who displayed her submissive attitude to Abraham's chief servant was ready to even follow a man that she has never met. She knew that marriage is for women who will be willing to feed their husband's horses and all that the husbands have. **This great woman did not choose to marry Isaac because of the promises made or because she was expecting her husband to be perfect but because she had made the choice before leaving her father's house to work out her own marriage by submission**.

The scriptures made it clear that when they were still afar off, she sighted Isaac in the field coming towards them and she asked from the servants who he is. The servant made it known to him that it was Isaac the man that will eventually become his husband. Rebecca then went on to come down from her horse and cover herself with her veil. What was she doing will be definitely the question on the lips of her servants; she was simply saying, I cannot carry who I used to be in my father's house into my husband's house. **She knew that no woman could succeed in her marriage by carrying her father's 'house' into her husband's house. No woman can enjoy a blissful home if she is not willing to forget about her achievements and the pride of her father's house.** Rebecca knew she must come down from her horse so that she can enjoy her new home.

Many women who are having problem with their marriages are having problems because they can't come down from their horses; they want to prove to their husband's that they know who they are, what they have and are not ready to let go of what they are holding on to. **How can you not let go of where you are coming from and get to where you are going?** Why will you put a new wine in an old wine skin and the wine skin will not burst. Let all the women who intend to have a glorious home get ready to come down from their horses and cover their faces.

Rebecca was simply making a statement, **she was simply saying I know nothing anymore except what I**

learn in my husband's house and I have nothing to hold on to, except what I have in my new home. So many ladies came to their husbands home riding on the horses of their achievements, educational attainments, exposure and riches; they have forgotten that the princess must forget her father's house if she will enjoy the king's desire and joy. **You can't import your past into your future and expect your future to be glorious**. Submission involves coming down from your horse and covering your face so that you can enjoy your home. Your fathers' horse will not guarantee your future; it is your decision to submit to your husband that will help you enjoy a glorious future.

God has not called women fools but it is important to note that only fools can have a glorious marriage. Everyone involved in marriage must be willing to let go of their rights and be ready to always agree so that they can build for themselves a glorious home. I remember an incident as a child of a friend who was always pushing our other friends to fighting, but when the fight starts he will run away and leave whoever his fighting to himself. That exactly is the picture of many women, they have friends who keep pushing them to fight and when the fight begins, they go back into their own homes sleeping. A wise woman will not allow any friend to push her out of a glorious home by pushing her to be at loggerhead with her husband. Submission from a woman is the key for a woman to enjoy her husband and build a glorious home. Submit to him.

CHAPTER VIII

Two Shall Become One

'***Therefore shall a man leave his father and mother, and shall cleave unto his wife; and they shall become one flesh....*** '

I have heard several preachers preached on the above verse of the scripture, but I feel there is a crucial point that the Lord wants anyone getting married to take note of. I have mentioned the need for anyone getting married to really grow up to maturity that he can leave everything behind him to cleave unto his wife. Yes, **cleaving will never happen until leaving has taken place.** That shows that becoming one which is the level that everyone that will enjoy marriage should get to is a process. **The bliss of a marriage or the fragrance of a sweet home will never be seen or perceived if the two do not become one and becoming one is not a magic that happens; it takes time.**

It is practically impossible to finish building a house in a day, there are processes that the building will go through and until the building is complete, it is still work in progress. **The tragedy of many broken homes is that many of them were not patient enough to finish building their homes. If you are having problems as you build, it simply means that you are still work in progress, that should not make you quit**. God has shown us the pattern for building a godly marital union and none of the processes can be boycotted.

It is impossible for a couple to cleave unless they have truly left everything they ought to leave behind and it is when that is done that they can become one.

The two have not become one at wedding; they shall become one as they build their blocks of union on leaving and cleaving. Interference from the past, from parents, society, friends and people who should not be involved in the homes that is been built has left many homes in ruins. I will love to emphasise leaving again because there is nothing that can work in a marriage when that has not happened. A man is called a man because he can take his decision and stand by it without anybody influencing it, but a child is still attached to his mother's breast. He cries all the time because he can't handle issues and until the parents attend to him, he will still be crying. Indeed, that is the picture of so many men in marriage, they are still babies, attached to their mothers' breast, they always run back home crying when things are not going the way they expect it to go and that is why they will be ready to break up with their spouse when anyone says so.

I visited a family recently and I was surprised to discover that the man of the house always returns to his home town and to his mother anytime there is a conflict in their home. He does not calm down until he has seen his mother and it is only the mother that can settle matters in their home. It is unfortunate that the mother is always excited to be the one the child is coming to; she is happy that her son has remained a child and has not yet grown up to become a man. The couple that will enjoy a beautiful marriage must leave where they are coming from and create their own world. Until they leave, they will not be able to build their own home. No matter what they see where they are coming from, they must realise that every home is unique. **The two shall become one is what the Bible says, not the three or the four.** So many people imported their past into their present and that is why their future is bleak.

I hope you don't mind that I am re-emphasising this point of leaving? It is the crux of the marriage that will succeed. **No marriage is immune to winds, storms and flood; it is the decision of the people involved that will help them stand together even in the darkest time.** If you have not truly left your father and mother, then you will think you have a place to go back to when the winds, storm and flood attack your relationship. I recently discover that many people that goes into marriage in our time often goes in with an exit strategy in mind and that makes it easier for them to find their way out of the marriage even with a slightest of challenge.

What does it take to cleave?

It is funny that it is just letter 'c' that differentiate the word cleaving and leaving; it therefore reveals that **leaving**

and cleaving are stages in becoming one and it is after one step is taken that the other stage begins. The desire of everyone that goes to the altar to be married should be becoming one at the long run and if that will happen there arc things that must happen as they cleave to become one. It is so painful that so many couple truly left but they never cleft to each other, so they did not become one at the end. It is impossible to just stop at leaving and expect to become one with your spouse; you have to be ready to move on to the next stage. Let me discuss briefly what it takes to cleave to becoming one.

Adjust

Adjusting is a major key in cleaving in marriage; **when people are not willing to adjust, they insist**. My wife and I have had serious misunderstandings and quarrels because the two of us insisted that we were right; these issues would have destroyed our homes. You can't cleave to your spouse and become one if the two of you are not ready to forgo your rights. **One major thing that you must sacrifice on the altar of a successful marriage is your rights.** To adjust means to alter, bend, amend, and change and sometimes to move in a new direction. How can you become one when the two of you want to stand on his or her right? The two of you may truly be right on issues but there are times that you allow the wrong to be regarded as right. **You must be ready to shift to meet your spouse at an equilibrium point.** Sometimes you have to bend or amend to be able to cleave to become one. Considering the fact that the two of you are from different backgrounds and have different orientation, you must be willing to adjust to the new life in marriage. You cannot be rigid and enjoy a beautiful marriage; you have to be ready to adjust. **Flexibility is the major key in adjusting to one's spouse.** If two different people from different backgrounds, world views and orientation will become one; they must be ready to shift grounds and adjust to one another.

Adapt

Another key factor in cleaving to become one as husbands and wives is the ability to adapt. I remember that as a secondary school student, we were taught in Biology class that animals have to adapt to new habitat for various reasons. **Marriage is like a new territory and an unfamiliar terrain for those in it and that is why the husband and the wife must be willing to adapt to the new life.** It is a journey that they have never embarked on, a path that they have never travelled before and an environment that they have never lived; therefore, for the two of them to succeed, they must be willing to adapt to one and another and to the new life that they have agreed to live. **Marriage is a decision to start a new world by abandoning the old; therefore, if anyone will succeed in it, they must be willing to trust God for wisdom and strength to adapt to the new life.** You and I have heard stories of marriages that collapsed because of the way the husband and the wife were used to using toothpaste. The marriage collapsed because the two of them were not willing to adjust to the reality that it is no longer about how they used to live and they failed to adapt to the new way of life that will suit the two of them.

Adaptation is the key to cleaving even after you have left your parents. If a man who loves going out end up marrying a woman who does not, if the two of them will live together as one and become one, they must be ready to adjust to a new way of life and adapt to whatever the decision the two of them will agree on. **The inability of the couple to adapt to the reality of their new world often spell doom for the home.** You have to get used to the fact that you are now joined to someone that sees things from another perspective and you have to be ready to settle into the relationship with that conscious decision that your relationship must work and be a blissful one.

Agree

The willingness to adjust and adapt makes agreeing easy for a couple. Many sweet lovers have become enemies because they could not agree and that is because they did not adjust to their new live and adapt to their new roles as husband and wife. Agreement is the secret of a successful cleaving in marriage; you have to always meet at the equilibrium point. The Bible reveals in Amos 3:3 that "two cannot walk together except they agree". **No relationship can succeed when the two of them are not in agreement.** The roles must be defined and practical agreement must be taken on all issues. It is impossible for any home to experience peace, joy and love when the couple cannot agree. The issue of unity is so vital that it determines the success and durability of any marital relationship; hence unity is possible when the husband and the wife can speak the same language and find a way to agree even when they have diverse ideas.

They were two before they decided to become one and they will only become one as they adjust, adapt and agree as an entity. The power of agreement in a marital relationship is what the devil hates to see being unleashed. **If one will chase a thousand and two will chase ten thousand, then the devil will fight any union that produces that kind of result.** Jesus even said if two of you shall agree as touching anything in prayer, that our father in heaven will grant it; that implies agreement also holds the key to answer prayers. Anywhere you see division, you will never see progress but when people can agree in love and are united in a course, success becomes easy to achieve. **Agreement does not suggest that they don't have differences or different opinions on issues but that both of them were able to come to a common understanding and were able to shift ground to move in the right direction**.

The inability of couples to agree is one major factor that contributes to the high rate of divorce in our generation. No home will succeed when the husband and the wife cannot have a meeting point on decisions and one of the reasons that often happen is pride. **All men have a measure of ego that they carry, while all women have inherent in them a level of stubbornness and rigidity; thus, these two attitude will never allow agreeing on issues possible.** In as much that the man is the head and that is the control panel of the body is, still the head cannot function independent of the head and vice versa. The head must find a way to walk in agreement with the body and the body must be willing to accept the control that comes from the head. Pride must be dealt with in any man that will succeed in his duty as a groom; sometimes the man must be willing to be the fool so as to achieve corporate success in the home. If any man and woman know that when they are united, it becomes easy for them to accomplish anything they set out to do, then the two of them will be willing to lay aside their pride and stubbornness to agree. The devil becomes a looser whenever he sees any marriage agree and move in unity.

I remember that there was a point in our marital journey that the Lord told me that **the greatest force on earth is a united marriage.** It was a period when almost everyone around me seems not to be getting along with me, when I was being misunderstood and I faced opposition everywhere I turn to; it was that moment that I discovered that my wife and I are the most important team on earth. **When you are in agreement, your burden becomes easier to bear. When you are united, it becomes easy for you to conquer any battle and climb any mountain.** The devil needs you to be in disagreement with your spouse so that he can be in control of your home and steal your joy away. Below are some suggestions on how we can achieve unity in our marital relationships.

1. ***Remember that you no longer own anything by yourself:*** As our wedding was drawing near, I wanted to access my wife's email account, she was my fiancée then. I needed to do that so that I can place a copy of our invitation there attached to some mails that we had agreed to send. So I requested for her password but she said no, claiming that it was her personal property and that she cannot share with anyone. I really did not feel bad about what she said until I took time to meditate on it. That was when I discovered the need that we should talk about the two of us not having anything of our own. I know that you might think that her email should be her personal property but why

should I have something that I cannot share with my spouse. The two of them were naked and they were not ashamed explained the scriptures; there is no way the two of us will agree when we both have our personal properties that we can't access. I have heard wives talk about their own personal money and husbands talk about certain things as their private life. You can't have a private life in marriage. You will find it difficult to agree and be united when there are certain no go areas in your individual lives. You can no longer have your own money or friends, whatever you have must be shared in all openness. **Anywhere you see 'I' all the time and 'mine' always, unity will be difficult to attain and love will be hard to come by. If the two shall become one, the word 'I' and 'mine' must be replaced with 'us' and 'we'.** This understanding is lagging in so many homes, which is why they are always at logger head on issues. I once told my children in the Lord who were preparing to get married to forget about the idea if the two of them are not willing to share all things in all sincerity.

My wife and I had to agree to ensure that we have the same friends. We know that we can have friends differently but whoever has chosen to become my friend has to be her friend too because she and I are one. **I can't have a friend who does not want to be my wife's friend and she can't have a friend who insists that he or**

she does not want to be my friend. We decided to do away with anything or anyone that will hinder us from always agreeing. If the purpose of marriage was for the two of you to become one, how then can you achieve that when you live in the same home as different entities? **It is not all about wearing a uniform or sleeping on the same bed and living in the same house, you both must recognise that you have nothing of your own again.** Whatever you once had before you got **married now becomes the property of the two of you. Let me submit here that it takes dead people to be happily married. You have to be dead to yourself and be ready to live for your home**. This kind of mind-set is what can make your home a heaven on earth. If marriage is likened to building a house and the two of you have agreed to build, how will you then succeed when the two of you keep the resources that you ought to put together in building your house? No one should have anything as his or her own anymore.

2. ***Remember that your marriage comes first in all things:*** I once asked a lady where she placed her marriage recently. She had explained that her marriage was in serious crisis because she is so busy at work and she does not have the time to attend to the need of her home. The matter of priority is a serious matter if we will ever enjoy a beautiful union in our

marriage. I have read and heard of several ministers of God whose marriages ended abruptly and those whose children became vagabond because the parents do not place importance on their marriage. In God's order, the second most important thing in our life after God should be our marriage but it is most unfortunate that people place their marriage as the less important matter of life. **Your marriage is so important that once you refuse to pay attention to it, then your whole life will be affected**. Your career is important because that is what earns you a means of living but your marriage is more important because that is what makes you to have the rest of mind to even make the money you seem to be pursuing. In decision making, before you consider yourself, consider your union. If you must disagree, consider the effect of the disagreement on your union. Watch out for those little matters that can become big issues in your marriage; always consider what effects your agreement or disagreement will have on your union. My wife and I got to that point when we have to let go of issues because we need to secure our home. **Your union is more important.**

3. ***Remember that you are both on the same mission:*** You cannot be in agreement when you find it difficult to remember your vision and mission from time to time. As I stated earlier on, if you both are on the same ship it is

because you are heading towards destination and if you keep that in mind it will help your decision making. Your husband does not have a different mission from yours, the two of you must work together to fulfil that mission. **Anywhere you see conflicts of interest, you will not see unity.** What interest you should interest your spouse, not just because any of you is superior or inferior but because of where you are jointly going. Whenever you remember that you both have the same focus, the same enemy and the same results to achieve, it will help you to always agree. One of the most shocking things I hear from couples these days is words like 'I have my life to live and my spouse has his or hers to live.' **Is it not strange that two people agree to build a house and invited people to be part of their decision, only for them to start and the two of them begin to tell people that individual has his or her own house to build, so they abandon the one that they should build that will give them satisfaction and joy later on.** In the name of career and success, so many homes have become battle ground. You may have your career but you cannot have a different mission in your home. The moment your career begins to conflict with your marriage then that career becomes the enemy of your home.

4. ***Remember that you will surely disagree:*** it was our final counselling session before we got married and

the pastor that was counselling suddenly asked us a funny question. He asked, 'have you guys been having misunderstandings and disagreements?' I laughed and so do my wife, because we almost disagree throughout our courtship period. But we were shocked when the man of God told us that he would not have joined us, if we told him that we have not been having misunderstanding. He made it clear to us that day it is the disagreement that made us to know what is sincerely on our hearts and to really adjust to each other; hence what is most needed as a quality is the ability to forgive each other before any offence. **Disagreement and misunderstandings should not be a reason for you to quit and break up your marriage; you must be willing to resolve it by your resolve to never hold the offence in your heart.** If indeed your union is crucial to you then you will always remember that your spouse is prone to errors as you do also. Your disagreement should help you to understand each other better and must be resolved almost immediately so that it won't degenerates to more heart-breaking crisis. In resolving your disagreements, you must avoid attacking your spouse's personality rather you have to address issues and that you must in love and gently. There is no home where they don't have issues to disagree on but it is the ability to handle them with wisdom that matters. In your becoming one, you have to learn how to agree from disagreeing.

5. ***Pray together always:*** It is a popular slogan that a family that prays together stays together; indeed, it is not just a slogan but the truth. Since the devil does not want you to succeed in becoming one, then you need to always ask God for wisdom to agree on issues. Of a truth you both came from different background and you are in a process of truly becoming one flesh, then you need the wisdom of God in building your home; which is what you must seek God for. A friend of mine shared with me that it is anytime that they want to pray in their home that a serious quarrel will come up and that he does not know why that was always happening. Hence, it was not just him that was experiencing such; there are many several marriages that experience such. **If your family can pray together then it will become easy to agree on issues and progress will be made with ease.** You have to make it a regular practice to pray together always as husband's and wife. In fact, holding hands in prayer strengthens the prayer of the husband and wife.

CHAPTER IX
Naked And Not Ashamed!

I was in a company of some elders one day and this issue was raised. One of them asked the others if it is wise for a man to tell his wife everything that is happening in his day to day affairs of life. I watched with rapt attention to know what their responses will be and I was not disappointed when almost all of them said that it was not wise for any man to tell his wife everything. Is that not the trend in marriages today? Is it not strange that two people living under the same roof, eating from the same pot and sleeping with each other, keep secrets from each other? I recently had the story of a woman who was always hiding money from her husband; she continued to do same to her husband even when the children were in need of anything. A few months later, the man needed money urgently and went to the pastor for help; the pastor knowing that the woman was doing well in her business asked why the man could not get the money from his wife, the man smiled and told the pastor that the woman does not have money. The pastor then told the man to come back after a few hours, while the man was on his way, the pastor sent for the wife and requested that he needs a loan of the same amount that the man needed and that she should bring it to the pastorium. The lady came at the exact time the pastor asked the man to come back and it was a thing of surprise for the same wife that told her husband that she had no money to come and hand over the money to the pastor. When I heard the story, I asked myself why? Why will two people who made a vow before God to be companions for better and for worse to end up keeping secrets from each other.

As I researched and see from the experience of people that surround me, I noticed several reasons that so many couples live in shame with each other and keep secrets. Adam and Eve became one as they lived nakedly with each other and were never ashamed. They were naked, they showed each other everything both their flaws and weaknesses and none of them were ashamed of each other but in marriages today, the reverse is the case. The following reasons can be deduced.

Firstly, many of the so called people that are getting married really don't know what marriage is all about and they have no understanding of what God demands of husbands and wives. If they do understand that they will know that no marriage can work when the couple refuses to be open to one another and be naked. Secondly, I discovered that trust is lacking in so many marital relationships, rather it is fear that is exhibited every day. **Anywhere trust is lacking, lies will prevail.** In many marriages where secrets are kept from each other, it is often because the couple cannot trust each other. Trust will definitely be lacking in a relationship fear prevails; I have heard several people say if you tell your wife everything then you are digging your grave and I have heard many of them said only a fool will trust his wife with every secret. Some are afraid that their spouse cannot handle information's accurately, that they will react instead of addressing the issues. Why do people lie to each other? **God hates lying and that is why one of the pillars of a successful marital relationship is the ability of the couple to live together with each other in honesty.** Thirdly, many marital relationships are not naked with one another because they allow people to influence them wrongly. They judge their own marriage based on what has happened to their friends or what the society is counselling them to do. I have heard many men say that they know that all women are witches and are evil; if you ask them how they come to that conclusion they will easily tell you it is because of the experience of people that they have seen and have heard. In addition, many people in marriage have allowed the devil to deceive them to think that they should not be open to their spouse. They have failed to realize that marriage can only succeed when it is built on God's principle and pattern.

The two of you shall become one if you are naked to each other on all issues, at all times and in all situations. One of those processes that will help you to achieve that state of union is to be truthful to each other and never to be ashamed of each other no matter the fault. Adam saw Eve the way she was, he saw her strengths, he saw her weaknesses and he was never ashamed. Eve saw everything about Adam also; he never hid his flaws from her, he never hid his fears from her nor his aspirations, he opened up to her and that was how they become one. That can also be seen in that the both ate the forbidden fruits, the man in his custom showed his wife everything that the serpent told him and they agreed to eat it. This is a key to success in marriage. Civilization seem to be becoming a curse to people than a blessing because people now throw God's principle away and try to reason for themselves why they should live otherwise. **You cannot become one with someone that you are not naked to. You have to tell each other everything, every time and everywhere.** The moment you begin to hide things from each other, the wall of your marriage is already cracked and the devil will gladly come in to destroy your home.

I recently discovered that many spouses started having issues with the issue of internet chatting. The influx of blackberry phones and smart phones makes it easier for people to keep having intimate friends online without the knowledge of their spouses. The danger is that many of the so called friends that they chat with begin to build affection unconsciously for each other and as the intimacy grows, an extra marital affair begins to grow. Why keep a friend that you can't tell your spouse about? You must be consciously open to your spouse if you will become one. You cannot be hiding things from each other and enjoy each other. Reject suggestions from people that will turn you against your spouse; let your spouse be your confidant. The moment it is easy for you to confide in some person apart from your spouse then you are at the verge of falling away and your home may collapse.

A decision that you must take as you enter into marriage is that there will be no communication gap and that there is nothing you will not be able to tell your spouse. If you can publicly declare before people that you are joining yourself to your spouse for the rest of your life, then telling your chosen spouse everything about your day to day activity should not scare you. There are so many homes that have broken up because of secrets that they have kept behind closed doors. The preacher in Song of Solomon rounded off his preaching by admonishing people to fear God because there is no secret that will not be brought opened. What you call a secret today will become news tomorrow and that is why you have to be plain with your spouse. Be honest towards each other and let nothing be hidden. We often counsel that every information that is necessary be shared about each other even before the couple gets married.

The Jane's story

A story was told of a popular journalist who had a very big wedding in one of the major cities in Nigeria, whose marriage got broken just a few weeks after the wedding. The wedding was such a big wedding that the high and the mighty in the society were in attendance but the news of their divorce rocked everywhere just a few weeks after the wedding. Everybody was eager to know what happened; the parents and friends intervened to see if they can save the relationship but the groom will not open up why he was willing to tear his bride apart and the bride has no idea of what she has done to deserve such from a man that she loved whole heartedly. The two of them have been friends since childhood but soon parted ways at some points between childhood and the youthful age. Nevertheless, when they met and decided to get married, they really didn't talk about what has happened in the past. The groom who also had a friend who has always been interested in the lady was already informed that the lady dated someone else when they lost communication but the groom did not ask the bride and the bride never mentioned it. Hence, on their wedding night, the groom was shocked that the lady was no longer a virgin; telling that to his friend who was not happy with the wedding in the first place, the friend saw that as an opportunity to ruin the relationship. He gathered vague evidences and told the groom that his bride actually was flirting around in the past. But the groom never opened up to the lady, he never told her why he was angry, he kept it to himself. It was the marriage was at the verge of breaking up that he opened up to his parents and pastor. Thus, the lady was given the opportunity to know what was in the mind of the groom and to speak for herself. The man soon realised his fault when he got to know later that his wife actually lost her virginity because she was an athlete and that she never at any time had sex with any man. Jane almost lost her marriage because she didn't open up before wedding about her past life and the groom almost made the greatest mistake he would have ended up regretting because he refused to open up and communicate everything with his bride. You must open the doors of communication and tell each other everything.

Communicate at all times!

Opening the doors of communication is part of being naked to our spouse. We must remember that **communication goes beyond just speaking and hearing. It involves listening to each other passionately and learning to express oneself without fear**. The communication line in so many homes is constantly dead and that is why the couple are not becoming one. God expects that the husband and the wife will be friends for life. Companionship that God wants in marriage is not just about the man having a helper but having someone that he can share life with. **You cannot be a companion to someone that you don't tell everything.** You must talk to each other and talk with each other.

In most relationships, they only talk to each other; they don't talk with each other. **Talking to someone has to do**

with telling someone what you want but talking with someone involves listening to the person. Communication in the real sense has not happened in a relationship when there is no adequate response to what is been said. It takes two people to communicate and **the real work in communication is listening**. Listening is not the same thing as hearing. Listening actually goes beyond hearing but involves hearing. Listening involves paying attention to what someone is saying with an empathetic attitude. It involves consciously paying attention to the details of what is been said beyond the words that are uttered. **If we are able to listen to one another as we speak, then we will be able to communicate better and be better friends.**

Many people find it hard to express themselves in their marriage because their spouse does not really listen to them and the fear of been misunderstood begins to set in. The option most people have chosen is to be silent but **when you choose silence in your marriage, the marriage is as good as dead.** You have to open the communication lines at all time; there should be nothing that you are afraid of telling your spouse. Listen to the heart yearnings of your spouse and pay attention to words that are not even uttered. We may hear things differently and that is why you will need to always ask God for wisdom so that you can speak the language of your spouse. Everyone has a language and an easy way to approach, find it in your spouse. Remember that she or he is your companion and your friend for life. If you don't communicate with your spouse then the society will communicate with him or her, friends will not communicate with him or her and most dangerously, the devil will use that space to communicate error to him or her. Don't allow your spouse to be alone in marriage, be the friend and learn to always open up to each other.

You should not be ashamed to have sexual intercourse!

The word sexual intercourse has been tainted by the devil in our society. Most of what is seen is sexual perversion and not the pleasure that God intended it to be. **Sexual intercourse is one of the processes by which the man and the woman become one; it is the seal of the covenant.** It is such a serious matter that Apostle Paul told the church that "anyone that sleeps with a harlot becomes one with the harlot". Whoever one has sexual intercourse with, one becomes one with. **God in his infinite wisdom and power designs sexual intercourse as a bonding process for two souls who have been joined together in marriage; he designs it for their pleasure.** Sexual intercourse involves an exchange, as the couple exchanges substances into each other and blood is involved. The involvement of blood makes it the highest form of covenant that God recognises. Through sexual intercourse procreation also takes place and that again is the desire of God for any marriage too.

Nevertheless, in many marital union sexual intercourse is not being enjoyed. While so many people are abusing sex, some others are not maximizing the purpose for which God intends it. Sexual intercourse should be enjoyed and that is the reason the couple have to learn to enjoy it in the right way. Several books have been written to help marriages on this aspect of the marital union; books like 'The Art of Marriage' by Tim Lahaye and the 'Model Marriage' by Dag Heward Mills sufficiently explained this important aspect of marriage. Husbands and wives should grow to enjoy sexual intercourse as they grow in marriage. Sarah and Abraham were seen enjoying this romantic expression of their marriage even in Egypt, Isaac and Rebecca also was seen enjoying that special gift of God in marriage. **Sexual perversion must not have a place in your home.** Learn and choose the styles that suit your spouse better and be creative as you desire to satisfy each other.

You are not permitted to deprive your spouse of this enjoyment in marriage. You should not be ashamed to talk about it among yourselves. You have to be sincere with each other on this aspect of your marital union; let your spouse know if you are being satisfied or not. Do not give room to tempt you outside your marriage, if you are not really enjoying the satisfaction of your sexual life, you must be free to talk about it. The only condition that can allow anyone to deprive his or her spouse is during prayers and that has to be by mutual consent. Nevertheless, the man and the woman has to live with each other in understanding that there are times that any of the party can be weak and therefore not able to have sexual intercourse. If there is a need for counselling about your sexual life, don't be ashamed to talk about it. You should enjoy your sexual life without shame.

It is a covenant and not a contract

The new couple has truly signed the marriage certificate but the certificate signed is not as important as the covenant that has been established before God and man. Only if most of the people getting married know that they have not entered into a contract on their wedding day but a covenant that God does not hold lightly. It is possible that most people who often consider divorce at any time they face any crisis in their marital life have forgotten that the marriage covenant is not breakable. God does not take the issue of marital covenant lightly because it reveals the kind of covenant that exists between Christ and the church. **Anybody can break out a contract but a covenant is deeper than that**. Solomon charged us in Ecclesiastes that we should not be in a rush to make vows because vows are always binding on those who made them. Most people on their wedding day do not pay attention to their wedding vows, that they made before God and those that attended the wedding.

It is strange that so many people don't know the power of the vows that they made before God on their wedding day, so they treat it lightly and handle it with levity. Hear what Solomon said in ***Ecclesiastes 5. "Guard your steps when you go to the house of God. Go near to listen rather than to offer the sacrifice of fools, who do not know that they do wrong. Do not be quick with your mouth, do not be hasty in your heart to utter anything before God, God is in heaven and you are on earth, so let your words be few. A dream comes when there are many cares, and many words mark the speech of a fool. When you make a vow to God, do not delay to fulfil it. He has no pleasure in fools; fulfil your vow. It is better not to make a vow than to make one and not fulfil it. Do not let your mouth lead into sin, and do not protest to the temple messenger, "my vow was a mistake.". Why should God be angry at what you have said and destroy the works of your hands. Much dreaming and many of words are meaningless. Therefore, fear God.'*** It is important for the new bride and the groom to pay attention to their marital vows and never forget that God hates people who do not keep their words. The marital vows that the couple exchanged on the wedding day must not be forgotten.

Those days will come when your marriage will be tested, when challenging situations will face you. Yes,

the wind, the storm and the flood will attack all marriages at different times. For some it might come as child bearing delay, for others it might be financial hardship. It can come in various ways, it might be sickness and pain at some point. Some families had to experience loss of children at some point and we may not be able to explain why. God didn't promise us clouds that will always be bright. He never promised us sunshine without rain. He never promised us roses without thorns; neither did he say that the road will always be smooth. **Test and trials of soul may come, but we must not forget our marriage covenant**. You said before the Lord, his angels and people that you will love care and honour your spouse at all times, in all situations and for better and for worse. Don't forget your covenant.

The popular TD Jakes movie "Not Easily Broken" depicts the reality that can face any marriage no matter how rosy and sweet it appears from the beginning. **We all pray for better days but what do we do when the hope for better days becomes glooming? What do we do when we hope for rain but all is hot around us? What do we do when friends become enemy and our dreams seem not to be coming true? What do you do when to feed becomes difficult and no help seems to be coming your way? Will you break up at such time? Will you abandon your vows? Will your covenants be broken just because of temporary situations and trials of life? Remember**

that it is a vow that you must be faithful to. Your vow should never be abandoned because God hates divorce.

The Balance

A young lady who was facing moments of challenges and troubles in her marital life was at the verge of breaking up with her husband. This beautiful lady once enjoyed a sweet relationship with her husband; they both were seen as a model family to the youths in the church as they display real affection towards one another. Hence, the storm, the wind and the flood arose as it would, but they couldn't just realise that what was happening to them was momentary and that their family was not just the only family going through such challenges at that time. She then decided to speak to one of the elders in their church who was married for forty-five years before his wife passed away. She wanted to know what they did in Elder's family that made their marriage to last that long. She asked this old man what they did that made their home a perfect marriage. The man looked at her and laughed; she was worried as to why the man will laugh at such a crucial matter when he knows that her marriage was at stake.

At that point, the elder answered her that she was wrong to think that his marriage was perfect. The lady was surprised to hear that, but the old man told her that their marriage went through moments of challenges, storms and flood but was able to survive because the marriage had a balance. **The marriage was far from perfect but was built on the truth**. The Lord Jesus was at the centre of that marriage and that was why it didn't crumble. That was the elder's explanation to the lady. He explained to her that the two of them had decided even before they got married to always look unto Jesus as their standard for everything they do; they decided to ask the question 'what will Jesus do?' at all times, when they needed to take decisions. Although Jesus was not married in the earthly sense but his lifestyle of kindness, goodness, sacrifice and patience was their standard at all times. The old man told her that there were times when they got to that point when they both felt that they will never be able to make it, but at such points, they remembered to look unto Jesus.

The truth remains that the Lord never told us that we will not face these challenges and whatever your family is facing, it is not peculiar to you. There are families who have gone through worse things than what you are going through and there are families going through things similar to what you are going through. Most importantly, how we handle the situations that we face in our moments of troubles and pain is what determines whether our marriage will survive the stormy period. Jesus must be the standard for your home if you will be able to survive the storms of life. Your marriage is likened to a journey and on the road, you must also expect that there will be rough paths, pot holes, bad weather, and uneasiness at some points but you cannot travel and succeed if Jesus is not in your ship. The disciples on their journey encountered the storm that threatened their lives, they spent their energy and wasted their properties because they thought they can handle it on their own but it was when they called on Jesus that the storm ceased.

Jesus is not a third party in your home and you must never treat him like that. He is the foundation on which your home must be built and he is also the only help that you can have when the storms of life ranges in your home. So many marriages have crashed because they felt they don't need Jesus to sort some things out, they believe that they should be able to reason things out themselves but my friend **Jesus is the only balance that every marriage need**.

He is the one that holds the vertical line and the horizontal line together; he is the meeting point for two different people in marriage. It is when they look unto him that they will see fewer faults in each other. It is when they call on him that they can have wisdom to resolve issues. He is the only one that can teach us to sacrifice our rights to stay married. We can see his example of patience, kindness and forgiveness as patterns for our marriages to work out. He is the balance that everyone needs in their marriage. Is your spouse changing negatively? Tell it to Jesus. No matter what storm is facing you, Jesus has the power to calm it and the strength that you need to go through it without giving up is in him.

As my wedding date was drawing near, my wife's Dad who I decided that I will also regard as my Dad, called me aside and told me that I must never call him to resolve any issue in my marriage. He told me that it is inevitable for my wife and I to have misunderstandings and crisis but I must never call on any man for the issues to be resolved. He pointed to the sky and told me that whenever you don't know what to do, call your heavenly father. Tell him everything, cry to him if necessary, complain to him and let him be the one to guide you in all situations. I am most grateful to him today for that wisdom that I learnt from my wife's dad; we have seen things that could have made us both to quit, but we resolve to always call on

There were times, when I was tempted to call it quit with my wife; there were moments when we both could not see any light at the end of the tunnel, but we called on Jesus. We know that many of those moments will still face our marriage but Jesus is the balance. Both the home that was built on the rock and on the sand was tested by the storm, the flood and the wind but the one that had the right balance never fell. Once it is built on Jesus and you allow Jesus to be at the centre of everything, then your home will not fall. **Let Jesus be your standard, look at him at all times; when you don't know what to do, why not ask 'what will Jesus do?' You must die to yourself and see Jesus as the governor of all your decisions**. There are times you will just say sorry, even when you are right; it is not about you anymore but about your home.

The fact that Jesus is the balance in your marriage does not mean that you won't be hurt by the one you love the most, it does not mean that you will not be angry when you are offended, it does not mean that you will not feel like pulling away from the one that hurt you, it does not mean that you will not make mistakes yourself, it does not mean that you will not have moments when you will pray and may not get instant answers but **it simply means that no matter what you will follow the Lord and not allow what you are going through to make you take the wrong turn**.

What will you do if you were to be Jesus when Judas betrayed him? What will you say if you were him when he was wrongly accused and condemned by the ones he loved? Will you pray for the ones that hurt you, offended you and despitefully used you or cursed them? Was it easy for Jesus to do all of that? Did he find it easy when peter denied him? How did he feel when he discovered that it was his trusted treasurer was the one plotting to betray him? He felt very hurt too because he was fully man when he came to the earth, but he always places the bigger picture ahead of the temporal pains. If you can ignore a lot of the things that makes you feel bad and look to making your home a heaven on earth, you can definitely save your marriage from crashing. Your spouse will definitely hurt you; he or she will offend you and sometimes will be insensitive to your needs but remember that **Jesus is your standard at all times.**

CHAPTER X
I Hate Divorce

'Another thing that you do: you flood the Lord's altar with tears. You weep and wail because he no longer looks with favour on your offerings or accepts them with pleasure from your hands. You ask, "why?" It is because the Lord is the witness between you and the wife of your youth. You have been unfaithful to her, though she is your partner, the wife of your marriage covenant. Has not the one God made you? You belong to him in body and spirit. And what does the one God seek? Godly offspring. So be on your guard and do not be unfaithful to the wife of your youth. "The man who hates and divorces his wife, says the Lord, the God of Israel, "does violence to the one he should protect," says the Lord Almighty. So be on your guard and do not be unfaithful.

Malachi 2:13-16.'

A popular servant of God recently told his church members that divorce is not a sin and that God permits people to dissolve their marital relationships when they are not fulfilled in them again. He told them several reasons that anyone should consider as reasons for divorce; as he spoke, the church applauded him in agreement to what he said. **What this pastor failed to tell his members that**

divorce contradicts the plan of God for marriage. I really cannot expect someone to speak the truth about something he has not overcome and that is a major reason that several people counsel others to divorce since that was how they solved their own marital crisis. But in the real sense, **does divorce solve marital crisis**? Most people that have broken marriages really were not able to fix their marital crisis and at the long run they still end up becoming a serial divorcee.

The debate on if it is proper for a man to put his wife away has been ongoing for a long time and even now the church has not been able to take a stand on whether divorce should be a way out of marital crisis or not. What is most alarming is the rate at which divorce is on the increase in this generation even among the people who ought to know the will of God on the issue. **One of the most common statements that I've seen is "Christians divorce at the same rate as non-Christians," undoubtedly giving the world another opportunity to shout "Hypocrite!" The non-Christians in the past sees Christian marriages as standards and examples to emulate but the rate at which Christian marriages now crash makes them to doubt us and puts a question mark on our sincerity. Most unfortunately, the church seems not to be able to agree on what is right or wrong about divorce. While some sees divorce as a practice that should not be mentioned or accepted among Christians, others believe that it is the best way out of conflicts.**

The Moses verdict

"When a man takes a wife and marries her, and it happens that she finds no favour in his eyes because he has found some indecency in her, and he writes her a certificate of divorce and puts it in her hand and sends her out from his house, and she leaves his house and goes and becomes another man's wife, Deuteronomy 24:1-2". The above scriptural passage is what many people refers to when they discuss the issue of divorce and just like the Pharisees once approached Jesus to test him on this same issue; they wanted to know if God permits divorce in marriage. They referred to the fact that Moses gave them the permission for marriages to be dissolved but they were shocked by Jesus' response. It is a possibility that a man find indecency in his wife or husband, but Moses recommended that for such a person to put his wife away, he must write her or him a certificate of divorce. Why did Moses not say that the person who wants divorce should just go ahead and divorce his spouse? Why is there a need for a certificate of divorce? How is this certificate gotten?

Moses wanted the Israelites to know that divorce should be the last option when they have tried all they could do, he asked them to get a certificate because a panel must have judged the matter before the certificate is issued and the deficiency in the spouse must have been proven beyond doubt. The women then suffered more based on this law because they were not even permitted to speak, the men therefore took the advantage to put away their wives for just any reason. **But JESUS said no, he refused to endorse divorce, rather he referred them back to the intention of God from the beginning which is for marriages to last as long as the couples are alive.** Divorce was never part of God's intention for marriage and that is still not acceptable to him for any reason. He told them that Moses permitted them because of the hardness of their hearts but according to his plan for marriage, divorce is not acceptable. Hence, if Moses permitted divorce, does God the initiator of marriage permit it? Jesus simply told them that Moses is not superior to God who ordains marriage to last through the lifetime of the couple.

Hardness of the heart, a major reason for divorce!

"It was because your hearts were hard that Moses wrote you this law," Jesus replied." Mark 10:5. **Divorce is a product of the hardness of our hearts; a man or woman that is stubborn, rigid and determined to have things his or her own way is considered to have a hardened heart.** Marriage is for those who are ready to adjust, adapt and agree; those who are flexible, who are correctable and are willing to let go of their rights most time. **Jesus in his great eternal wisdom showed us the root cause of divorce**. In the beginning that Jesus was talking

about, Adam and Eve had not yet eaten the forbidden fruit, they have not abandoned God's garden of glory for their own ambitions, so they had their marriage raw and it was built on a divine pattern of love, nakedness and acceptance. Adam saw Eve the way she was, she didn't hide anything, Eve saw everything about Adam and they lived accepting each other and enjoying their union; **but when sin came, all of that was lost**. We started making choices by our reasoning and we started struggling to accept the way God patterned things to be. We started rejecting his order and started mapping out our own way. No one wanted to follow God's pattern and plan for marriage again because now we can see and we are now in charge of our lives. *"from the beginning it was not so"*, was the master's reply because he actually was the beginning of marriage. **Moses only gave them what they wanted because they have chosen not to follow God.**

Let me illustrate this with the story of Joseph the earthly father of our Lord Jesus. He was set to marry Mary when he discovered that she was pregnant and that alone is enough to put her away, but he chose not to do it the way other men were doing it. He didn't want to put her to shame or be cruel towards her, so he chose to do it privately. While he was planning on how to do it, the angel of the Lord visited him and commanded him not to because the lady was carrying a special child. Was that instruction easy for Joseph? Several questions must have run through his mind; he has relatives to explain to. Nevertheless, he chose to obey and keep the marriage. Put simply, his heart was not hardened although he has a just reason to put his wife away. **Anyone that hardens his or heart does not see things from other people's eye, he or she always insist on having his way**. Joseph was no such man, he let go and let God have his way. **Men like these were not common in those days and even in our time they seem not to exist. It is such men that can marry and enjoy a lasting home.**

In a generation where everyone wants to always be right; when what God says no longer matters to us, divorce definitely will be definitely prevailing. **Marriage is for those whose hearts have been softened and pierced that they can easily accept God's will, admit their imperfection, willing to always forgive, adapt to their spouse in all situation and adjust to be a better person.** It is not for those who are not willing to bend or give way to other views. It is when this hardness of our hearts have been dealt with that we can submit to God's will for marriage, enjoy our spouse and bring the best out of our marital relationships.

Is it not pathetic that those who walk to the altar to get married these days carry hardened hearts? They have no place for God in their hearts and that is why it is difficult for the woman to submit and the man to love. **It takes a man who has been broken to love the way Christ Jesus loved and a woman who is broken to submit the way God commands us to**. That kind of love cannot sit in a selfish heart, it cannot sit in an ego filled heart, it cannot sit in a proud heart; hence that is the only kind of love that can build a marriage that will not crash. How many men can still love their wives if the wife was to be in Mary's state? **Divorce will continue to prevail in our generation because most of the people in marriage still carry this hardened heart.**

In most divorce cases, the lawyers involved often find a way to resolve the differences but when they find it difficult to, that they resolve to give them the certificate of divorce. Do you really want to know why most of those issues could not be resolved? Hardness of the heart! **How can you resolve an issue when the both parties are not willing to shift ground and agree?** The cross shows us that we cannot live our lives the way we want and fulfil our destinies. if Jesus does not cross us and if we refused to surrender to meet him and accept him to take over, we will not live a fulfilled life. The horizontal line must meet with the vertical for it to form a cross; **how can you harden your heart and enjoy marriage**? The nature of a hardened heart that we inherit from Adam must give way to the nature that God intends for us to have from the beginning, which is the nature that can be controlled and guided by the Spirit of God, if we must have a successful and an enduring marriage. It will be difficult for a man or woman whose heart has not been touched and softened by God to forgive even before the offence is committed.

A hardened heart will not just forgive; he or she will also keep the record of wrong. A hardened heart will never consider the joy of the spouse above itself; a hardened heart will be filled with jealousy and bitterness. This is the case for divorce and anyone who does not want to travel that path must be ready for brokenness and ensure that he or she does not choose someone whose heart is still hardened. **That can only be possible when you allow Jesus to guide you because the heart of a man is deceitful above all things and desperately wicked.** Divorce therefore was an option for those who do not want to follow God's pattern of marriage. It is the way out for those whose hearts are hardened towards God's principles of marriage. **Divorce is for the arrogant and the stubborn people, who are not willing to adjust, adapt and agree**.

Let no one put asunder!

Jesus saw the opportunity in the test of the Pharisee to redefine marriage and to correct them about divorce. Up till that time, the people believed that divorce was not a big deal just like we do in our days also, but Jesus the one that started the beautiful institution of marriage decided to re-establish his unchanging counsel for marriage. *"but from the beginning it was not so, from the beginning God made them male and female. For this reason, a man shall leave his father and mother and be joined to his wife, and the two shall become one flesh, so then they are no longer two, but one flesh. Therefore, what God has joined together, let no man separate".* **Mark 10:6-9.** Let me point out the issues that Jesus spoke about in his response: **first, he wants them to know that nothing has changed the pattern that was set at the beginning. The Ancient of Days cannot become changed by the changing times and events, his principles remain the same.** Moses may give them the permission to divorce because of the hardness of their hearts but that does not make it acceptable. It is possible that divorce has become an acceptable trend in the society, it might have become an easy route out of marital problems and the majority have come to agree to it for several reasons; yet the initiator of marriage said no. Nothing will make Christ Jesus accept divorce as a way to be accepted in marriage, even if it is popularly accepted, it does not change the unyielding purpose of God.

God will not bend his standard for any reason; that standard of marriage is unchangeable. Divorce is not part of it. Situations will happen in marriages that will challenge the relationship; still God wants the marriage to remain as one. **Secondly, the response reveals that marriage is for a man and a woman, not for a man and a man or a woman with another woman. The woman was made as a companion to the man not as a companion for another woman; and vice versa.** In a world where people's hearts are hardened, Jesus made it clear that the order of God on marriage remains a union between a man and a woman. **Let anyone give excuses or suggest reasons for having a companion of the same sex, which does not change the truth that God hates it and it is an abomination to him**. Christ Jesus reaffirm again that marriage was never an institution where a man will leave apart from the woman or where a man will find companionship in another man, the creator made them male and female. It is quite strange that so many people that claim to know God do not live in conformity to this eternal truth; the woman was not made for herself, she was not made to live on her won, she was not made to just have kids; rather she was made as a companion to a man. **The creator made them male and female explains the Lord. We must not allow ourselves to be deceived by this changing trend and demonic inventions on marriage these days, God has the final say and it is written boldly in his word. Marriage is a companionship between a man and a woman, yes anything apart from that is perversion.**

Thirdly, the Lord Jesus went on to emphasise the issue of a man leaving his parents and be joined to his wife, so that they can become one flesh. Again, **the Lord was affirming here that becoming one is God's ultimate desire and that is only possible when the couple has left everything to cleave to each other.** They shall become one as they follow the principles, he gave earlier which is to leave everything and stick to one another.

Can anyone break what God has joined?

The Lord Jesus declared to those Pharisees that 'therefore what God has joined together, let no man put asunder'. Do you understand what this means? **It means that it is God that joins people together in marriage**; whenever anyone is joined together in marriage whether in the church, court or anywhere else, God is the one that joined them together. Yes, they are responsible to take the decision to be married or who they want to be married to but because marriage is solely God's own idea, God is the one that joins them together. **The parents may be involved, the church may be involved on their wedding day, the society and friends may also be involved but it is God that will join them together as one.** If you take note of the tone of the Greek words that Jesus used when he said therefore what God has joined together, let no man put asunder, you will discover that the Lord was not suggesting to them, he was given them an express command that no man should attempt to dissolve any marriage. This is where I am always scared when I see people try to play certain roles in breaking up of marriages; no one is permitted to dissolve any marriage because they are not the one that joined them initially.

Jesus was seeing here giving an order that **no man has the right to separate any marriage**. It does not matter who the person is, no one is permitted to separate any marriage. There is no permission for divorce. **What the lawyers can ask them to do is to live apart but they cannot break the spiritual bonding**. Their becoming one is both in the flesh and in the spirit and even if it is possible to give them the permission to be apart in the flesh, nobody has the authority or audacity to separate them in the spirit. **The conclusion was drawn there as the Lord Jesus made them to know that even if Moses had given them the permission to write a certificate of divorce and gives them an option of to put him or her away; Jesus the author and finisher of marriage forbid it. Why is it forbidden? It is the Lord that joined them together**. Once a man enters into marriage vows and covenant with any woman, the two of them must never forget that God is the centre of that marriage and no one can separate them. Let the lawyers give the certificate, yet no one can separate what God has joined together. He said that he is the witness between the man and the wife of his youth, so it goes beyond what any of them just want. It is possible that you are tired of each other and desperately want to stay away from each other, you can pack out and throw your wedding rings away, yet God has joined you together. **It is only when you can undo what God has done that you can divorce.** I hope this explains to you how much God does not approve of divorce. He hates it with passion.

He might not force you to stick to his will but his intention is clear. You and your spouse should stick to each other till death do you part. **The certificate of divorce cannot end your marriage; it is God that joined you together.**

Your choice!

One of the issues that confront us as humans is that we are free to make our choices in life. God will never enforce his will on us and that is why divorce becomes a matter of choice. He has shown you his pattern for building a successful marriage and there are evidences all-around of us of the consequences of not following the pattern; still it remains our choice to either stick to that pattern or not. God has revealed it clearly that no marriage can work when the couples have hardened heart and they are not willing to agree, but he will leave the choice to us to make. "You will hear a voice behind you telling you this is the way to go" was what the Lord said through Prophet Jeremiah but the choice to listen to the voice that you hear is completely your decision. God has provided enough guidance for us on the issue of marriage, starting from our choice of life partner to living a successful marital life, but how many people are adhering to that guidance? Hardness of heart indeed a major factor in making marriages collapse. God ordained that marriage will endure the test of time and that the couple will live together as long as they have life but most people that get married in our days go into marriage with an exit strategy in mind; they were never ready to stay in the marriage in all seasons. Is that not a choice that they have made for themselves? For them, marriage is not for better and for worse, it is for better and better. They never turned their doors to wall when they made their marriage vows; rather they kept their doors opened waiting for a time when they will be willing to get out of the marriage. They have forgotten that **at some point in marriage everyone will have reasons to want to quit but it is those who can endure at that moment that can succeed in marriage**. It is so strange that we now have marriages that did not even last a week because those that were involved believed they can't cope with someone they just got married to. In the cyc of a lot of people marriage is a contract that is signed by two people, that has an exit clause should in case any of the parties involved are not interested in anymore. They fail to see marriage the way God sees it; therefore, they redefine marriage in their terms.

Shanti Fhendalhn in her newest book, The Surprising Secrets of Highly Happy Marriages, Shanti compiles some stats and conducts some research of her own on marriage, and specifically, what makes for a happy marriage. Her statistical findings, and the implications of these findings, are fascinating. Here are a couple of stats that I found to be particularly interesting as it relates to faith and marriage: 53% of Very Happy Couples agree with the statement,

"God is at the centre of our marriage" (compared to 7% of Struggling Couples). 30% of Struggling Couples disagree with the statement, "God is at the centre of our marriage. "She writes, "Highly happy couples tend to put God at the centre of their marriage and focus on Him, rather than on their marriage or spouse, for fulfilment and happiness". It is therefore important to note that any marriage that is not built on the true foundation of God's purpose for marriage and that is not sustained by the principles that he mapped put for building a godly home is definitely at the risk of crashing when the wind begins to blow. God has no intention for married couples to come to the point when they will think of breaking their marital vows.

Hope you have not forgotten that the devil hates your marriage and for me, **divorce is a direct attack on marriages**? If God established marriages for companionship that brings fruitfulness, then the devil will be happier to see this purpose not come through; one of the ways he does that is to make the couples in marriage believe that their marriage cannot work no matter what and that it is better to stay apart than work on their differences. He knows the power of the two who are united versus just one who lives in pain of loneliness. Relating with people can be very complicated at times and marital relationships that is not well grounded on the true word of God will fall victim to the lies of the devil; whose aim is to see those homes tear apart so that they will not bring glory to the ones that establish it. **Divorce is an aberration and you must not allow the thoughts of it succeed in your mind no matter what your marriage goes through.**

Infidelity is one major reason that people seeking divorce often gives as a reason for seeking it but many fail to realise that God has refused to give up on several of us despite of our unfaithfulness and unrighteousness towards him. My mentor once told me that **there is no innocent party in a divorce; where there is a will to mend things, there can always be a way**. Trust can be broken, we can be disappointed and at times betrayed by our spouses but that is still not enough a reason for us to quit our marriage relationships. I know someone reading this might probably be thinking that I am not been realistic on this issue but as I consider marriages of old, I see couples with determination to stick with their spouses even when they are hurt and offended. Most of those couples never believed in going out of their marriage even when their rights were being trampled on. For many of them, divorce is a thing of shame and that resolve strengthened them to stand in the face of any marital storm. That is unlike our generation that couples already have their minds made up on quitting when tired and fed up.

I am not sitting in the place of a judge to condemn those that are involved in divorce but to stand on the plan of God for marriage which does not involve divorce. **I am baffled at the lack of determination in couples these days to**

weather any storm; I can't see their resolve to stand for their marriage. They are so weak that any little matter brings up the issue of divorce. In Genesis 31, Jacob called his two wives and told them that he was willing to run away from their father but I was shocked to hear the ladies say what part or inheritance do we have in our father anymore? They showed their resolve to stay married to their husband even if he has problems with their father; they were not willing to stay back because they have already made up their minds before they got married that they will remain married to Jacob no matter what. Rebecca never had an exit strategy nor did Sarah at any point thought of partying ways with Abraham even when he was making stupid decisions. What has happened to that resolve in couples today?

Moses only permitted the Israelites to divorce not because it was the right thing to do but because the people were not willing to obey God and follow his principles of marriage. Moses had no authority to redefine what God has defined but Moses gave them the permission because the people were not willing to stick to God's plan and they suffered the consequences greatly. So many people want to use the Moses' permission as an excuse for them to also put away their spouses but that is not an excuse to wilfully disobey God because God does not bend to any man's standard. Let me briefly share with you from the above text the stand of God on divorce.

Divorce turns you against God

God categorically made it clear to the Israelites that the reason that he had stopped answering their prayers was because they had been directly violating his command. They attend church, pray and fast regularly, they even bring offerings and tithes before the Lord but the Lord has decided not to pay respect to any of those things. He does not even want to relate with them because they are violating his plan and principle on marriage. The intention of God was that they become one with their spouses but they are not abiding with that desire, rather they go about living unfaithfully with their spouse. They have forgotten that marriage is a covenant and that God has been serving as a witness in their homes to see if they will keep to the vows that they made to their spouse. God does not take the issue of marriage lightly, which is why he himself is the witness in every marriage. He sees everything that you do to each other; he sees it when you refused to keep your promise to care for your spouse, he sees it when you maltreat the person you vowed to love. If God hates unfaithfulness that much, then he abhorred divorce a great deal. He does not want unfaithfulness in marriage, he wants people to stick to their covenant and be steadfast in upholding the promises that they made to each other. God specifically declares that he hates divorce and it simply means he hates the people who are involved in it. Divorce is like sabotaging God's effort to make our homes heaven on earth. God never promised that marriages will not go through storms and floods but that in the midst of it, they must learn what it means to sacrifice self and stay in love towards the erring partner. If we must please God, then we must be willing to learn from the way he relates with us. If God were to break away from any man that he cannot condone then he must have broken away with us all. God accepts us in spite of our errors and that is a major principle he expects us to learn from him as we stick to our partners. God is unhappy with anyone that put his spouse away.

Happy, strong marriages are definitely possible, but it takes work—an ongoing effort. We're all sinners who need a Saviour, and when you put two sinners together in a relationship like marriage, it's bound to be difficult sometimes. Our sin supplants sacrifice with selfishness in our marriages. If we want to experience marriage as God created it to be, a reflection of his sacrificial love and leadership of the Church, we've got to keep him at the centre of our marriages. Your spouse isn't your Saviour, Jesus is. Live that truth and your marriage will more likely thrive. **You must never forget that God hates it when you decide to put your spouse away because he wants you to relate with him or her as lovers for life. Your love should not end because things are not going your ways.** Marriage is not about who is right or wrong, it is about been ready to sacrifice our rights sometimes to protect our relationship. God hates unfaithfulness and it is when you stay faithful to your spouse that you display true and sincere faithfulness to him. It is possible to be unhappy in marriage for several reasons but breaking up such marriage is not an option to resolving the issues causing the unhappiness.

God sees divorce as cruelty

I want you to pay attention to this verse as rendered in the New Living Translation ***"For I hate divorce!" says the LORD, the God of Israel. "To divorce your wife is to overwhelm her with cruelty," says the LORD of Heaven's Armies. "So guard your heart; do not be unfaithful to your wife.*** Divorce to God is an act of cruelty and such acts God detests and does not take lightly. Permit me to translate this scripture in my own word; I will simply say that to divorce your spouse makes you a wicked person, no matter what you give as reasons for it. It is indeed cruel to push your wife or husband away when you have vowed to be there for him or her at all times, in all seasons and situations. **You didn't marry your spouse because of his or her perfection, you definitely knew that he or she had weaknesses when you choose and assured him or her of your unfailing**

love; how cruel then it is for you to now put such a person away? If you see divorce the way God sees it, you and I will agree that we are not permitted to see it as an option in resolving our marital crisis.

Divorce tears the lives of the people involved apart even if they pretend to see it as the only way to be happy. It is not just cruelty against your spouse; you are also being cruel to yourself when you divorce your spouse. Is divorce really an option? Is it truly the way to become happy? It is never the way to resolve issues. No matter what storm you go through in your marriage, you have to choose to resolve things rather than accepting this ungodly way of resolving things. Malachi the prophet made it clear that the reason God has stopped answering the prayers of the people and has refused to look on their gifts and offering with honour is because of their act of cruelty towards their spouse. I hope that explains the severity of divorce to God. He turns deaf ears to the prayer of the people involved. God sees divorce as the peak of betrayal and the cruelty receives silence as a reply. Let no one paint divorce for you in the light that God did not paint it, no matter how popular it has become, it is an act of cruelty. Whenever anyone divorces his spouse, he betrays God's trust and cannot earn the favour of God. The Almighty God sees your partner as one with you in flesh and spirit and that is why he frowns at the cruelty of anyone who decides to put his partner away, thereby breaking the bond that God is involved in.

Paul the Apostle also made this clear to the Christians in the early church. He made it clear that even if someone marries an unbelieving partner, it is still not a basis for divorce. The unbelieving partner has already become one with the person and the person can only hope that by his or her own godly conduct can help the unbelieving partner become the person that God desires him or her to be. **Marriage covenant is deeper than people understand, it is not to be treated with levity, and it is not to be entered without the understanding of its implications and consequences. Who you marry and how you marry the person becomes irrelevant after you are married, because the choice has been made and the covenant is unbreakable.**

Consider your children!

"And what does the one God seek? Godly offspring"

In a movie that I saw a young couple were having serious problems understanding each other, so they decided to live separately with the woman taking custody of their son. They continued to quarrel anywhere they meet and cause scenes that embarrassed the child each day. On this fateful night, the boy went to the church and vandalised the church auditorium; he did not just do that, he also wrote the word 'liar' on the church building. The pastor on seeing this, he sent for the parents and asked them what they were doing to their child. They began to argue again and then the pastor told them that their child is becoming who he is becoming because of what they have done to his world. They have virtually turned God to a liar in the eye of the innocent boy, because he has prayed to God to help his parents resolve their problems, but to him God did not answer. This couple never truly realized that they were not just ruining their own life by their separation and divorce, but that they were also destroying the life of their child who is already becoming violent and angry at God. Have you really considered your children before taking the decision to break up?

The task of bringing up godly seeds and training them to become all that God desires them to be is a major task that God has given to couples. **God wants marriages to produce children and not just producing children but to train them to be godly**. This should serve as consolation to any couple that is having difficulty in having children; it is the Lord's desire. He wants you to have children, God is expecting godly seeds from you, therefore in due season He will cause you to have children. Hence, this task of training children to be godly is such an important assignment given to couples by God and this can be seen all over the scriptures. This task demands the ultimate and best of parents. Wilfred and Francis Tyler illustrated that a child is completely blind mentally, socially and spiritually; that does not mean that a child is blind physically but that the child is like a clean slate "tabula Rasa" on which the parents, society or environment writes on. **Parents are therefore expected by God to rise up first to the task of writing something godly and reasonable on this clean state, in order that the lives of their children may be appreciable. But what becomes of these children when their parent divorce?**

There is no doubt that when parents who are actually supposed to write on the clean slate are divorced, such children will be affected. While parents neglect their children and run after wealth and their personal happiness, they expose the children to damage from the different experiences they see around them which are morally wrong because there is no one to tell them what is right or wrong. **The home which is the root of the child plays a major role in sharpening his life and it should be noted that everyone is a product of his background. The absence of a parent in the nurturing of a child is like a major leakage in the roof over the head of a child.** The Bible clearly stated that the Israelites were given a mandate to teach their children the law of Yahweh. It was expected of them to teach their children the fear of the Lord, they were to nurse them and instil in them the wisdom and knowledge of God as stated in the scriptures. (Deuteronomy 4:9-10). The children are expected to learn these things from their early age in life but what becomes of them when their home is broken and the parents live separately from each other. **When parents are in different places, the lesson of love, unity and peace that the children are to learn from them becomes impossible since they should have been the children's first examples in life**.

The peaceful and harmonious living of two parents reflects the loving nature of God and the church; all these are supposed to be taught to the children in the homes. **The children will learn to respect others as they see their parents respect one another**. The truth is that when parents are considering divorce, they do not call on the children in their discussion and some do not care for the children after the divorce. This makes it so crucial for the couple considering divorce decisions to consider the plight of their children after taken the decision. It is often more hurting for the children to see their parents break up. **Children often react to their parent divorce in several ways and many of them develop ungodly behaviours**. These behaviours that the children develop do not often come to the surface immediately. The effect of divorce on the children can be seen in the following ways:

1. **Physical Effects**: in order to discover how divorce affects children physically, we must understand that the children's reactions to divorce vary with

age. Children within the age of six through twelve slowdowns in their physical growth and motor development. All children are conscious of what happens around them and their appearance; they acquire self-esteem when they are looking good. Their feeling of worth will help them in developing positive work habits and skills that will be useful in life. **Divorce affects children physically as there will be no adequate care by both parents. Most of the children react to the announcement of their parent's divorce with apprehensiveness or anger. Several of these children panic and begin to experience a stunted growth.** They end up lacking personal attention to guide and control them when they get involved in physical activities. The physical attention and provision needed from the parents are not there. And in the case when the children have to stay with the relatives of their parent, the result is that they do not have all that they need to grow well. Due to financial problems, the physical growth of the children becomes affected. Because of where they live and service financial needs, the children become stressed and there are situations when the children need to leave school to do menial jobs to survive the financial challenges. It is not only financial crisis that these children faced; they also go through physical loneliness. **They face physical insecurity in the**

absence of their parents even if they have step parents. They become very lonely even in the crowd, the fear of the future grips their hearts and they faced educational difficulties. When it comes to educational achievements, children living with their parents do significantly better than children from non-intact families.

2. **Psychological effects:** There are many psychological aspects of a child's life that change when parents go through a divorce. **A child may not show initially how he or she feels about the divorce, but the true feelings of that child eventually surface. Children incorporate repertoires of angry, impulsive and violent behaviour into their own behaviour as a result of observing their parents' response to frustration and rage.** This is something that many children that witness the divorce of their parents go through. The children naturally look to his or her parents' example of how to handle certain situations and emotions. During divorce, much anger and aggression are expressed by one or both parents of the child. This is not healthy, for the child sees that example being set by the parents and begins to react in similar manners to life issues. **Anger and aggression tend to become the child's tool for**

solving his or her problem. The child becomes like his or her parents and could cause harm to others because of not knowing or understanding how to control these feelings. In older children and adolescents, events of conflicts had the largest and most consistent impact on their adjustment, with intense conflict leading to more externalising (disobedience, aggression, delinquency) and internalising (depression, anxiety, poor self-esteem) these are symptoms in both male and female children. Depression is a major psychological effect that divorce has on children; this is not something that occurs during the divorce but has major effects on the later life of the child. When a happy life of a child is suddenly interrupted by parents ending their marriage in divorce, the world of the child transforms. Their reliable safe haven called home turns into a sumptuous place full of fear, doubt and confusion.

3. **Emotional effects:** As children grow and develop, they gain better control of their emotional feelings. It is home, school and community that teach a child how to express his or her emotions. But the most important of all is the home. Hence, when homes break, children lack parental love and this makes them emotionally stranded. In their view to express themselves, they

get attached to the wrong people. If a child lives with criticism, he learns to condemn. **If a child lives with hostility, he learns to fight. If a child lives with divorce, he learnt to be shy. If a child lives with shame, he learns to feel guilty. If a child lives with tolerance, he learns to be patient. If a child lives with encouragement, he learns confidence. If a child lives with fairness, he learns justice. If a child lives with acceptance and friendship, he learns to find love in the world. And to conclude the gem one may say, if a child lives with divorce, he may learn to divorce later in life.**

Recently a leading crown court judge sparked controversy by claiming that many offenders come from single parents' families. The Judge John Curan in BBC News United Kingdom told a youth conference on crime that single teenage mothers' often made bad parents. The fact is however that all too many of those who end up in the criminal justice system do so against a background of an absent parent-usually the father. Parents must realize that children took priority in a relationship and they had to learn to stick together. When children do not enjoy love, belongingness, self-esteem and security, they tend to join groups where they will enjoy what they want. This is why a bulk of children in cultism and prostitution come from broken homes. Divorce affects children emotionally as they lose self-concept and self-respect as they face social or cultural stigma. **Divorce makes children to be depressed, guilty and anxious. They tend to blame themselves for their parents' decision for the divorce and they become anxious of the future. The shock of a divorce can numb a child's feelings. Teenage and premarital sex is one of the results of emotional in-balance resulting from broken homes.** These children in their hearts seek to be loved but think that the best way is to become sexually active.

Nicole Martin said that children from broken homes are twice as likely to have sex before the age of sixteen, the legal age consent. She confirmed report that around 25% of children of divorce or separated couples said they had engaged in under age sex with only 13% of teenagers whose parents are married. Where there are disturbances in a family, children feel rejected and they look for love and stability in the wrong way and place. They mistakenly believe they will find these elements in a partner through sex. The vast majority especially girls, deeply regrets what they have done and suffers emotionally. Another challenge is cohabitation among young people. When children of broken homes could find no emotional joy at home, they prefer staying with the boy or the girl that they think can give them joy.

4. **Social effects:** Every child is usually sensitive to what others think about him or her. They are evaluative of people's responses to their action as they evaluate other people's speech and action. In order to have proper social relationship children need to develop the concept of healthy self-image. This can be achieved when children have positive identification with their parent. They are denied this in divorced marriage. Divorce makes children build low self-esteem; they see themselves as inferior to others as they try to be known, they get involved in crime. So many children from broken homes find it hard to relate with other people; they may have discovered to pick up unwholesome attitude as they watch their parents live in confusion. Divorce affects girls socially. Research findings shows that some girls later in life do not accept their gender roles and may have difficulty in sexual relationship. Some girls do not know how to behave around boys since they lack father's presence as the role model. They may grow up to be excessively seductive when around boys because they have not learned to properly with the opposite sex. The rate of teenage pregnancies and

abortions which has become a social problem could be linked to broken homes was the assertion of the new research on married parents and crime. Some young women find it hard to get married because of sadness and fear of similar disappointment. They find it hard to keep their promises. If a child does not stay with their parents, they may later become societal problems to the society.

5. **Spiritual effects:** Spiritual growth in children is a process that includes internalizing values taught and displayed by adults, especially parents. The basic spiritual development at the primary school age is the development of conscience, morality and values. They develop through interaction with adults. They progressively move from one stage to another. At the children stage, all children generally love God and love to worship him, they also want to do what they think he wants to do. They believe in prayers and can pray sincerely. They have the ability to understand that they are sinners and to know God's plan for their salvation. Hence, children become judgmental when they see something different from what they hear from the scriptures. 33% of children learn their religious beliefs as they see their parents practice them. **For children to grow spiritually they have to be taught**

by their parent and that is impossible when the children are absent. Spiritual values can be developed in children as they see it around them as they imitate what they see. Christian parents are responsible for the developments of their children spiritual life as they share bible stories but as they ultimately display what they taught the children in their day to day living. **Divorce affects children spiritually; to children who believe that God loves them, they may find it difficult to relate to a God who did not make their parents stay together**. If the child loves to pray, he or she may struggle with the fact that God did not answer his or her prayers for their parents to remain married. Divorce destroys children's confidence in God; though it may make some draw closer to God for comfort, companionship, provision and assurance of better future. Some children may turn against God in anger and frustration. Many divorcees run back to God through prayers, participation in church activities. As children follow them to church, they may be close to church but their interpersonal conflict destroys their confidence in God. Children of divorce homes often end up in bitterness against God and the society.

My friends, as you consider these devastating effects of divorce on the children, is it therefore possible for God to approve of divorce when he wants godly children from marriages? **How can a home that is thrown into confusion, tumults and chaos produce and train godly seed?** Divorce is not just an act of cruelty to the parties involved, it does more damage to the innocent children involved in such marriage. In my personal experiences as a child that grew from a broken home, I am able to identify with the frustration and pain with the reality of the background I came from. So many of these children's future gets completely shattered by the parent's decision to divorce and many of them never recover from the hurt of what their parents did. **God wants godly seed from marriages and that is only possible when the parents live godly themselves. Divorce destroys this agenda and makes many of these children completely hostile against God**. Most of the parents often lost their right to correct the children as the children have lost regard for them since they were not able to resolve issues in their marriage.

These children often suffer in silence with no one paying attention to them; while the parents are nursing their hurts and are seeking for their own personal happiness, the children are thrown into untold confusion. They end up living between two worlds as they try to take a decision on who to stay with. **Many of these children end up losing confidence in the institution called marriage. I have discussed with many children from divorce homes and it was shocking to discover that many of them do not want to marry because they don't**

want to end up like their parents. God has revealed in the scripture that children are his heritage and they are so important to him like arrows are important to a warrior; therefore, he does not take lightly the issue of parenting. Parents must always remember that children belong to them and he has given them to the parents as a trust that they will be required to give account off later. Divorce is completely against the will of God and He will not look favourably on anyone involves because of the children from such marriages. Couples should not just consider their selfish desire for happiness when they chose to end their marriage, they should consider their children and remember that the choice that is to be made may end the glorious destinies of their children.

It really does not matter what anyone thinks about divorce, the truth remains that the devastating effects of divorce is much more than the advantage that the couple hope to get by quitting their marriage. Divorce damages not just your own life but the lives of your children and that should make you consider working on your marital differences than choosing to break up your marriage. There is no marriage that can't work, if we are willing to make the necessary sacrifices needed for it to work. You and your spouse are to be friends for life and misunderstandings are inevitable in your relationship but your willingness to resolve them will save your home from crashing. No matter the storm, your marriage can survive and it should survive. **Don't give up on your marriage, don't be unfaithful to your spouse, remember that God is the witness in your marriage and you will give account.**

CHAPTER XI
The Fire Must Not Go Out!

My wife just joined me in Abuja where our church is located; a few weeks after the wedding she needed to return to complete her thesis in school. On her arrival, she started her national youth service corps at the heart of the Abuja city. I have made it a duty to call her when she was in school several times in the day, but I did not feel it was necessary to do that anymore since she was already at home. Even if she goes to her place of assignment as a youth corps member, she will definitely return home; therefore, I care less about calling to check on her as I used to do while she was in school. On this fateful day, I noticed that my wife's countenance was not bright and all my effort to make her smile was not working. She was looking so sad, angry and was withdrawn; I couldn't bear looking at her that way because I know that she is not herself. I quickly took her inside to find out what was visibly wrong with her; in amazement she said 'I noticed that you don't really love me anymore'. 'Why will you say that? Why will I stop loving you?' was my response. She said, 'of course you have not been calling to check on me like you used to do before; now you can go the whole day without asking after me once. I believe you now have other things that have taken your attention and I am no longer important to you.' I sincerely did not see any big deal in what she said until I noticed how serious she was on the matter;

she has concluded that I am already changing just like many men used to have a changed attitude in marriage which is less affectionate to the way they used to behave when they just got married or while they were in courtship. I had to take my time to explain to her that I have not stopped loving her but I know the explanation did little or nothing to her opinion except I start calling her the way I used to before.

Yes, I have changed, I have become passive and have started assuming that it does not matter anymore whether I call her or not. I have forgotten how that calls has strengthened our intimacy. I had not stopped loving her but I was on that route unconsciously because **when you refused to feed your love life, it begins to burn out.** The assumption that we don't need to continue what we used to do for our spouse is a dangerous signal that we have become passive towards our relationship and if we do not wake up, we might not know when we have allowed an unusual gap to exist between us and our spouse. **The reason many people enjoyed a beautiful and loving courtship was because the two of them worked on making their flame of love burning every day, they were willing to impress each other every day and they were willing to go out of each other's way to resolve issues; but most people abandon those things in marriage.** It was not that God has not made them choose the right person but that we have often allow expectations to hinder us from taking responsibility for our relationship. I thank the Lord that my wife did help me to see that I was becoming a different person, I might not have known and I will assume that I still love my wife. My friends, we don't love in words, we love in deeds. It is when those deeds stop that it becomes evident that we have stopped loving our spouses.

Work In Progress

The joy of getting married is often short lived when there is no understanding of what it requires to sustain it and stay married. Nevertheless, no matter how much you have put into your marriage to ensure that it is well established, you cannot stop at that point and maximise the purpose of marriage. Permit me to say here that **your marriage begins to die the moment you stop feeding it with the necessary foods.** Yes, **wisdom will help you in building the house, understanding will help you in establishing it and making it last but knowledge will help you in furnishing the house for maximum enjoyment.** If I spend my money on building a big mansion and I worked very hard to establish it, there will be nothing to enjoy in it if I do not furnish it with all that we need for our own satisfaction and peace. Let me emphasise again that the desire of God is for you to enjoy your marriage, this is why you have to fill your marriage with all that will make you enjoy it. Hope you are not feeling bored by this truth because there will be nothing in that building if it is not filled with the best of the best? **It is the things that you filled your marriage with that you will enjoy and that is what will make your marriage your home.**

In my interaction with so many young couples, I have come to discover that many of them are battling with what they call 'this sudden change' in their spouses. The fear that love do vanish in relationships after wedding makes them to be suspicious of every little change that they observe in their spouse. Is this not a legal fear? It is definitely true that in many marriages, the affection and intimacy often drops after wedding and this is because many of the couples have forgotten that their fire of intimacy and love will start quenching when they stop working on it. **The assumption that the wedding day is the ultimate in the marriage life and that once they are married, everything will fall in place by itself has crippled so many marital relationships.** As stated in the previous chapters that no man can lay the foundation of a building and stop working and say that he has finished building. If the wedding day is likened to the foundation laying ceremony, then there is no resting until the building is complete and not just for the building to be complete, they must continually work on maintaining it.

God commanded the priest that they must never allow the fire to go out of the altar; day or night they must ensure that the fire is burning on the altar. He told them that they must remove the ashes every day and add fresh wood every morning, so that the fire will continue to burn on the altar (Leviticus 6:12-13). This is quite a symbolic and important message for couples. Love is regarded in the scriptures as flame or fire (Song of Solomon 8:6-7) and no one can just start a fire and expect it to continually burn on its own. If the fire of love and intimacy will continue to burn in any marriage, there are principles that we must learn from the instructions of God to the priests. God intends that marriages will enjoy deep intimacy forever, He wants the couples to be lovers for life and to be companions that will never leave each other, but that can only happen if the couples will not just sit down and expect things to happen but if they will be ready to follow the principles that will be discussed below. The fault that the Lord pointed out about the church is that they have forsaken their first love (Revelation 2:4) and that is a major issue that is causing so many marriages to crash. **We cannot start a fire and expect it to burn on its own without our constant supervision and sacrifice; why then should people start a marriage and expect it to work out on its own**. What must you do to ensure that the fire never goes out in your relationship?

1. **Take away the Ashes of Yesterday:** The priests cannot make new fire on the altar of God with the ashes of the fire that they made yesterday still remaining on the altar. If the fire will continue to burn, they must remove the ashes of yesterday's fire. The ashes of yesterday's fire will not allow the fire that they are to make today

to burn well and bright, so it must be removed before the priests will start the fire for the new day. **The ashes of yesterday's fire are garbage's and leftovers of incidence that happens in the yesterday of our marital relationships; our fire of love and intimacy that we hope to start today will not burn if we do not take them away.** This is such a crucial matter in marriage because in many homes where you see conflict, you will also see the inability on the part of the couples to throw away the issues of yesterday; they are always carrying the ashes of yesterday around. If your fire of love must be burning day and night, you must learn to let go of whatever happens yesterday. **Don't bring the ashes of yesterday's fire into the fire that you are making today. You and your spouse have to become perfect forgivers and never allow the pains of yesterday to destroy the joy of today. There is no way you will have fire yesterday and not have ashes, but you will not be able to have fire today when you cannot take away the ashes of yesterday.** This is so crucial to the fire of love in your marriage, you must learn to let the errors, mistakes, pains and issues of yesterday pass with yesterday, you must not bring them into a new day in your home. You and your spouse will surely have ashes every day and if you both can't handle it, then you will find it difficult to have true happiness in your home. **You must be ready to**

let the issues of yesterday pass with yesterday, stop recounting the offences of yesterday, you cannot keep the records of the ashes of yesterday and enjoy today. You have to stop looking backward if you must go forward. There is no future in the past. Yesterday is in the tomb and it is only fools that sit on the grave of what happened yesterday and hope to experience something new today. You cannot experience a new thing when you are not ready to forget the things of old and stop remembering them. You have to stop remembering the past so that your home will experience newness. **Your marriage should always experience a new level of intimacy and enjoy the excitements of creativity. Stop allowing the ashes of yesterday to destroy the joy of your today.**

2. **Add New Wood Every Morning:** The priests are not just to remove the ashes; they are also expected to add fresh wood every morning. They must realise that God does not want a repetition of the same experience of yesterday; he does not want the fire of yesterday to be on that altar today, he wants them to add new wood so that they can have a brighter and purer fire each new day. The new wood must be added in the morning after they have removed the ashes, so that they can start every new day with freshness. What does this imply to our marital relationships? **Our homes must experience newness every new day, we cannot just**

remove the ashes of yesterday, and we must be ready also to add new things to our relationship. There must be creativity, if we will not be bored and tired of each other. When we wake up every day, both the wife and the husband must wake up first to remove the ashes and then be resolved to add newness to that relationship. Our homes will experience greater joy and excitement when we deliberately add new woods every morning. **No one should wait for the other person to do it, the two of you must be resolved that your daily experience in your marriage will be unique and exciting.** One major concern that I see in most relationships is the issue of tiredness, being bored of one another and irritation. All these are bound to happen when there is nothing new added to the fire of your love. **We as humans get tired of the things that we do the same way, over and over again; there must be creativity and freshness in your relationship.** There must be a conscious decision from the couples to make their homes a new atmosphere of exciting romantic events every day. As you live together, you are bound to discover new things about your spouse. The resolve to make your home have a new atmosphere of love will help you to enjoy an exciting marriage every day of your life. **Try something new on all fronts, deliberately do something new with each other, don't get used to the same way of doing**

things and ensure that you avoid staleness in your marital experience. You must make your home an exciting place to come to, you must show your spouse something new every day and be deliberate about it. Choose to make your spouse happy in a new way. If all you can do is send a text message to your spouse, send it in a unique way. Make your relationship special each day. **Doing something new entails that you are not doing the same things that you used to do before and that should be your watchword in your marital relationship.** You must add new wood to have fresh fire every day. It is impossible for you to have a lamp that will keep burning if you are not ready to add new oil, in the same way you cannot enjoy a marriage that glows in love when you are not ready to add something exciting to your love life. It is important to also be willing to add new wood to your sexual intimacy in your marriage; you have to be willing to work on doing new things to enjoy a better sexual intimacy in your home. So many couples become so lazy in this aspect of their marital relationship, that they unconsciously give opportunity to tempt their spouse; you have to be creative in your sexual intimacy. **Everyone gets tired of doing the same thing, in the same way, over and over again; you and your spouse must be willing to add something new. Go the extra mile to make each other happy**. Let the happiness of your spouse become your priority. Add new woods, don't just stick to the same wood; make your home fresh every day, say things differently, dress differently, go out of your way to make your marriage colourful.

3. **You must not get tired:** The Lord demands that the fire on the altar must never go out and that is the responsibility of the priests. They are to ensure that the fire must be burning on the altar both day and night, which implies that they have no excuse for the fire to go out at any time. My dear friends, we have no option than to ensure that the fire of our love keeps burning. **We might feel tired at some point but we must not forget that a moment of no fire is enough to crash a marriage**. It is the responsibility of the couple to be committed to making things beautiful in their marriage daily. The day when you feel the fire is going out and you don't know what to do, is the day when you need to cry unto God for help and remind yourself of the beautiful experiences that you and your spouse have had before. **Your fire of love and intimacy will keep burning when you add the woods and you do it continuously. You have to add the wood of communication, openness, forgiveness, and kindness continually. You have to remember that as you take the ashes away daily, so must you add wood and as you add the wood, you must also check that the fire is intact from time to time.**

Don't fall into the error of assuming that things are always right in your relationship. Watch out for your spouse, look after him or her, pray for him or her and ensure that you don't overlook what needs to be fixed. Check from time to time the state of things in your home. Speak with each other on the state of things. My wife and I do set a few days apart to talk about the state of things in your home; don't just assume that things are alright. I once sensed that my wife was not looking so excited, she was getting angry at every little thing and was easily irritated; I didn't take that for granted, I instantly spoke with a marriage counsellor that I know can speak with her. She came back better and stronger. I remember that the marriage counsellor told me that if I have not taken note of her, I might have lost her to depression. **Pay attention to your marriage my friend by paying attention to your spouse. In a world where marriage is fast losing its value, you can keep your marriage and enjoy your spouse for as long as you both shall live.**

Excuse me sir, I think I have lost my first love!

I once had an interaction with an honest man who told me categorically that he believes that he has lost his passion for his marriage. With tears on his face, he told me he couldn't conceive how things have gone that bad, that he really does not want to see his wife anymore. He has lost the excitement of seeing her, he has lost the passion of being married, he does not need his wife to tell him that he has changed, and he knew that he was no longer the same man that he was before. He now prefers other things to spending time with his wife. Sometimes he travels out just to be away from his wife and that was the situation things are with him as he shared with me in a heartbroken state. I once had a man said that my wife now irritates me and I really don't get excited about her anymore; in the same vein there quite a lot of women who are just looking for a way out of their marriage because they no longer feel the way they used to feel about their husband. The question often remains why.

Why do people forsake their first love for their spouses? What are the things that kill the sparks and passion that once existed in a loving relationship that they have suddenly become enemies? Is it normal? One of the excuses that you hear from couples is that they don't have time anymore because they now have children and other things that are now occupying their time. It is crucial for us to note here that the moment a man or woman losses his or her first love for the spouse, then the relationship is on the edge and it is just a matter of time before the relationship officially expires. I have always been wondering as to why relationships that were once fulfilling suddenly become a thorn in the flesh of the couples.

Firstly, the ability to accept the truth is the greatest key to restoration. No one can seek something that he does not accept that is lost. So many people like that my friend have lost it but they are not sincere to themselves that they have lost it. You have to be truthful to yourself that things are no longer the same with you in your marriage. You need to be willing to accept that you have lost your first love, your passion and excitement for your marriage. My mother once told me as a child that, the greatest evil I can do to myself is to deceive myself. It does not matter who is deceiving you, you must not deceive yourself. You know the truth about yourself, you know how far things have gone bad in your relationship and it is in accepting this truth that you can be restored. **Secondly, remember where you have fallen.** You must be able to identify where things went wrong in your marital relationship. There is nothing anyone can do for you if you cannot identify where things went wrong. For Elisha to help the sons of the prophet to recover the axe head, they need to tell him where it fell. **You must be able to also identify where things went wrong. It is possible that things fell apart of the issue of money, or sexual intimacy or relating with the third parties; you must be able to identify where it has fallen.** That was what the Lord told John the beloved in the Island of Patmos to tell the church in Ephesus, they must remember where things fell apart before they can be restored. I counselled that my friend to truly discover and remember where the marriage started leaking. Are you going through a similar experience and you are desperately crying that God might help you fix things; my friend you need to know where exactly things got messed up. It is good that you know that things have fallen apart but you must know where it fell. You can't go to a doctor without you knowing exactly where you are feeling the pain. Discover it and then let's talk about fixing it. Be honest to yourself in this evaluation because it is what will help you to resolve issues.

Thirdly, repent. My friends, restoration starts with repentance not shifting of blames. We must be willing to accept our faults and errors if our first love and passion for our spouse will be restored. Yes, your spouse might have offended you but at this juncture when you are in need of restoration, you need to look beyond the person that offends you and deal with the issues. **Accept that it was wrong of you to have become irritated of your lover, accept that you have offended God by breaking your vows and that you were drifting away from your marriage. You need to be humble enough to accept that you were at fault on the issues that caused the loss of your love and passion**. God will be willing to help you when you are ready to repent and ask him for mercy. Moreover, you are not just going to ask God only for mercy, you need to ask your spouse for her or his forgiveness too. You need to confess to him or her, the truth of how you have been feeling about your marriage. You can't hide your deepest feelings from the one you love and even at the time when you seem to be filled with hatred towards him or her, you must tell him or her, the truth. **It is in speaking the truth that your restoration will begin. We are not immune to falling and making mistakes in our marital relationship but our willingness to repent and ask God for help is what will save our marriage.** In repenting, we must cry to God for help so that the devil will not succeed in tearing our marriage apart. At our moment of falling away, it is possible that we are already tinting towards having extra marital affairs, we must not hide it, and we must confess it and turn away from such relationships.

Lastly, we must be ready to return to doing the things we used to do before. Love can only be characterised by the actions taken and not in terms of promises made. **If you have truly repented, then you must be ready to return to doing the things you used to do before. Start relating to your spouse the way you used to.** You must let go of your errors and rise up to your responsibility. All that you need to do to earn the trust of your spouse again and to make your marriage work is to return to your duties of love. Be the man you used to be or the woman you used to be. Do the works you used to do at first; that is the sign of restoration. Most of the couples that I have had the opportunity of counselling have complained about the fact that their spouse suddenly stops being the person that he or she used to be and most often than none it is because there were certain things that they used to doing before but the spouse has stopped doing.

Hence **all that is needed to convince that spouse that you have repented is for you to go back to doing those things. Those things no matter how little they are have served as sparks in your relationship and if your fire of love must keep burning you have to continue to do them**. I never knew that my wife appreciated the text messages that I used to send to her daily until I stopped. Repenting is not just about stopping the wrong things that you used to do but also about starting the right things that you used to do but that you stopped before.

It is certainly true that we can get lost in the midst of our daily activities and the numerous tasks that we have to accomplish but we must be able to commit ourselves to ensuring that we consistently do the things that will help our homes to become the homes that we desire. **We must always remind ourselves of the fact that when we are done with our numerous tasks at work, the home remains the only place we are to return to**. What then becomes of you when you have allowed your ambition and desires for success at work to make you ruin your happiness at home? **You can have achieved great success at work but if you fail in your marriage, your life will be miserable because your work cannot give you what your marriage was purposed to give you.** Therefore, if your fire of marital bliss will not go out, you must be ready to always do what is necessary to keep the fire of love burning.

What is too big for you to give to ensure that your marriage remains a heaven on earth? The joy of marriage and its bliss is not expected to end after just two years of marriage but it should continue till death do you part but that depends on your willingness to keep the fire burning. One shocking discovery is that people are supposed to understand each other the more, love each other more and become happier with each other as they spend more years together but the reverse is the case. It has been discovered that most couples grow apart as they grow together which is not supposed to be. The first year of marriage is often referred to as the honey moon stage of marriage, the second year to the fifth year is seen as the discovery and decision stage of the marriage, while the relationship that survived at the discovery stage enters into the next stage of gradual loss of excitement as the reality of raising children and sustaining the family begins to take the centre stage of the marriage relationship. Hence, so many marriages lost their fire completely at this stage as they allowed the duty and responsibilities of raising their children to quench the fire of love and reduce the commitment that they have towards each other. Most couples at this point stopped caring for their spouse and began to pay attention only to the needs of their children. The lack of caring attention towards the spouse will definitely expose the spouse to friendships that might in turn leads to the end of a marriage that was once blissful. **The fire must keep burning at every stage of** your marital life and it is not God that will do that for you; you must be ready to put conscious efforts into ensuring that the fire must not go out.

Why do couples often forsake their first love?

1. **Assumptions:** I recently discovered that so many of us in marriage often assume that once we get married everything will automatically fall in place. We assume that the most important stage of our relationship is when we were still laying the foundation for our marriage, which arc the courtship stage and the wedding day. We put in so much effort to see that we stay committed to each other at the courtship stage and we were willing to spend our last penny to ensure that the wedding day is successful; after which we believe that all must go on well in that home automatically. **If many of us in marriage put in the kind of hard work, passion and commitment that we put in our courtship into our marriage then our homes will be blissful; but we are often assuming that it is no longer needed for us to do anything to sustain what we have started.** How can you plant a seed and after it germinates, you assume that it will grow on its own and bring forth fruits without you taking time to clear the weed and do all that is necessary for the seed to grow and bring forth

fruits? Why do we stop working on our relationship at the wedding stage? Why do we stop paying attention to those things that we used to do that brought happiness when we were in courtship? Costly assumptions that can destroy our marriages are what we must avoid **if our fire of love will keep burning. There must be continuity! Be willing to keep doing those amazing things that you were doing when you were in courtship and see how beautiful your home will be.** Many people have asked that what happens to love after wedding, I simply tell them that the people that were in love before wedding stop nurturing their love, they stopped working on those things that made them both happy, yet they expect a miracle to happen daily in their marriage.

2. **Negligence:** The fact that most couples assume that all will be well in their marriage after wedding is not just the only error that we make but most of us at that stage also begins to neglect our spouse and no longer pay attention to what makes him or her happy. The height of any marital relationship is not wedding, wedding in itself as I said earlier is not marriage and it will never be the determinant for what happens in marriage. There are people who did not have an expensive wedding or a big wedding but have happy homes while there are people who spent all their efforts on making their wedding day memorable but are living memorable pain every day of their lives. If a man

is overjoyed because he lays the foundation of his house and neglects all that needs to be done to ensure that the building is completed, he should be considered a fool. **You must pay attention to every detail that can make your marriage sweet and make your spouse happy**. Remember that **your happiness is in your spouse's happiness**. You cannot afford to be negligent from that moment on. You have said I do and the time has come for you to do all that you have promised to do. You made those vows before God and men to do certain things for your home to be filled with joy, you cannot therefore expect your fire of love to be burning brighter and hotter every day when you have refused to do those things that are needed for you. The little things that matters must not be neglected. **You have sown the seed, so you must be ready to pay attention to the little things that that the seed needs to germinate grow and bring forth fruits; or else you will have nothing to show for it in the future**. Stop saying that it does not matter anymore, it matters ad it will continue to matter as long as you want a happy home. The seeds of love in your marriage must be daily nurtured. You must daily pay attention to the needs of your spouse and consciously do things that will make you both happy.

3. **Expectations**: Norman Wright in his book explains that when expectations are not met in a relationship,

they lead to frustration which eventually leads to anger. **Marriage remains an empty jar, it is what the couple bring pour into it that will be there. God is not responsible for your marriage so do not expect God to come and fill the jar up for you.** It is your duty to fill the jar with love and respect. You are the one to ensure that you put the right thing in the jar because what is in the jar is yours. It is just like sowing seeds, you cannot sow maize and expects cassava fruits or most importantly it is not possible for you to sow anything on a piece of land and expect it to bring forth produce. The only thing that land will bring is weed which can be called troubles in marriage. What are you bringing into your relationship? If your fire of love will keep burning and it will never go out, then the two of you must be willing to add fresh wood every day. It is a daily assignment! **In as much as you are not assuming that your marriage will automatically work out as a miracle and you are not neglecting your duties then you must also be ready to do your part and not just expect everything to happen from your spouse.** It surely takes two to tango and if one party is not willing to do anything then nothing will be achieved. The two of you have to get to work every day to ensure that your marriage is achieving the purpose of God. **You both have to be willing to sacrifice daily so that the fire will not go out.** The flame of love should be always blue and not red, but it can turn red when the necessary woods are lacking. You must be willing to bring something amazing, exciting and wonderful into your love life every day; that is the only way you will enjoy your home till death do you part. **Always remember that the day you stop, that is the day it ends.**

4. **Unforgiving Attitude**: One of my friends published a book recently on forgiveness and that helped me to discover that many people that claim to have forgiven other people are still stuck in the past. **You cannot have a marriage where there will not be misunderstandings and offence because you are in a process of becoming one**. That process will take time and endurance; therefore, you must be willing to forgive your spouse even before the offense is committed. He is bound to offend you even as he tries to ensure that you both have a glorious marriage, it is your ability to overlook those offences and endure the hurt is what will help your marriage to work. Marriage is the coming together of two imperfect people who have decided to love each other unconditionally. **If you cannot forgive and let go of your pains, then you will be the one deliberately sabotaging your efforts to keep the fire of love burning**. This is a decision that you have to take and you must stick by it. Forgive forward, forgive always, do not keep the records of

wrongs and let it be registered in your consciousness that you too make mistakes. It is when the two of you can forgive each other without calling in the third party that you are matured enough to keep the fire of your love burning. **Whenever you insist on not forgiving, you are deliberately collapsing what you have been spending years to build.**

5. **Not for Better, For Worse**: Will things ever be rosy in our life? Are we always going to find things easy? Will the sky always be blue? What of the time when the sky will be dark? Will there always be food on the table? What happens to your fire of love when you go through fire and storm? Will the storms of life quench your fire of love? **One truth that we must accept with all conviction is that our journey in life will not always be smooth. There will be trying times in our marriages and that is just the fact. The rain will fall, the wind will blow and the storms will rage no matter how much you work to keep the fire of love in your relationship**. Nevertheless, such moments are to help you renew your vows and strengthen your chords of love. **Moments of pain are times when the true strength of our love and commitment should be revealed.** If the fire of love will keep burning in your relationship, then you must be ready to enjoy both the good times and the bad times with your spouse.

There are spouses who left their partner when things were going wrong, this shows that they were never really in love with their partners and they lacked the understanding of what the covenant of marriage is. What will you do if your wife experiences delay in child bearing? Should you blame your spouse for the sudden loss of your child? How do you react to that ugly moment of life? That is not the time for you to trade blames or get angry with your spouse; you must be willing to go through all the different seasons of life together. Remember that there will always be rainy season and dry season; winter and summer, spring and fall. Whatever season you are going through in your home, just remember that no season is permanent but your love for each other must be permanent. If you set your spouse as a seal upon your heart and as a seal upon your arm, then many waters will not be able to quench your love. A seal cannot be removed; in the same vein no challenges of life should be able to wash your love for your spouse away. **The joy of marriage is in staying with our spouses not just when things are wonderful but when things are ugly.** That is the only way your fire of love can keep burning. Stick together in prayers and remember that there is no situation that is greater than God. Let the Lord see the sincerity of your love for your spouse at all times. A few years ago, I know of a great man of God whose wife suffered insanity. This man of God did not disown her but rather loved her, took care of her and ensured that he was always there for her. That is the kind of response that God is seeking from you and I in our marriage. **We must be willing to show the commitment needed at the time when our partner seems to be going through the heat of life**. Don't allow the fire of love to go out because of the unpleasant situations of life

FILL THE ROOMS

Proverbs 23:3-4 "By wisdom a house is built, and by understanding it is established; And by knowledge the rooms are filled with all precious and pleasant riches...."

I know you have been asking since you began to read this part on what you must fill your marriage with. There two rooms in every marriage. The rooms must be filled with knowledge and I will briefly discuss what these rooms are and what they must contain.

1. **The Upper Room**: One of the truths that this book has tried to establish is that marriage is God's own innovation and if anyone has hopes of sustaining it and enjoying it, God must always be involved. The chord of three cannot easily be broken says the preacher and

that means that in any relationship that has God at its centre, no matter what happens the chord of that relationship cannot easily be broken. He is the only one that has the wisdom, knowledge and the understanding that the couples need in building a blissful marital life. Jesus made this clear when he talked about the foolish man and the wise man; while the foolish man built his house on the sand, the wise man built his house on the rock. **It is only the house built on the rock that will not give way when the storms, floods and winds of life begin to blow and only God is the rock that your marriage must be built on**. Therefore, the upper room must be kept for your family to interact with God daily. **That is the place that you and your spouse must meet with God from time to time, it must always be filled with prayers.** When everything seems to be going wrong and you don't know what to do, that is the room you must enter and pray until your joy is full. **Wisdom says that any marriage that will work must be built on God, sustained by God and you must never allow anything to make you abandon the upper room.** You must always keep that room clean and when children begin to arrive in your marriage, you must always take them there and teach them the secret of that room. **That is the engine room of your marriage; it is also the power room of your home and the strong room where your treasures can be**

protected. If the devil can stop you from entering the upper room constantly then he is about to crash your marriage and steal your joy. The upper room is not a room to be visited occasionally; it is the room that you must enter every day, if the fire of your love will always be burning. I hope you understand this secret?

In many homes, they have no upper room, they have no time of interacting with God in prayer, they neither take time to hear from the throne of grace and mercy nor do they keep the prayer line with God open, therefore when the devil attacks them, they have no one to defend them. My dear friends, marriages have always been under attack and the devil will not rest until he sees our marriages fall apart but we must run into our secret place to be shielded and protected. David told us this secret when he said that "he that dwells in the secret place of the Most-high will dwell under the shadow of the Almighty". The upper room is the secret place of the highest for your family and it is not a room you visit occasionally. You must constantly go there, take your family there every day. The devil hates it when families pray together.

2. **The Bed Room:** The bedroom has been described as one of the rooms that have caused many homes to break. **This is the place where the couples are**

meant to enjoy sexual intimacy and romance in their marriage. God designed that couples in marriage enjoy sexual pleasure and be happy but the reverse is the case in so many marriages. The devil is successful in turning the bedroom to a dirty room and the room where so many destinies of great marriages often ends. The couples are to enjoy sexual intimacy with each other in this room without shame and secrets. They are to fill this room with romantic love and be willing to share everything without reservation. Tim Lahaye in his book The Art of Marriage extensively dealt with this aspect of a marital relationship because many couples are ignorant of the truth about sexual satisfaction in marriage. **It has been revealed that when the couples do not enjoy sexual satisfaction, they are left opened and vulnerable to sexual temptation.** In this room, the couples ought to enjoy each other and make every moment vulnerable. The couples must not be forced or be unwilling to release themselves for their spouse for maximum enjoyment. Paul the Apostle explained that the only reason that anyone that will excuse himself or herself from sexual intimacy must do so with the consent of the spouse and it must be for consecration to seek the face of God. I have heard funny stories of marriages where a particular spouse will tell the other that sexual intimacy always must be according to his or her terms. **There must be**

agreement and the couples must not be selfish, the two of them must be satisfied and that is the key to a fulfilled sexual life. You must be willing to talk to your spouse about your sexual life; you must be sure that he or she is getting satisfied and if you find out otherwise, you must be ready to seek help. The man must understand that it takes more time for a lady to be satisfied than for the man, so he must be patient. **The man must understand the complexity of his wife's sexual desire and must be ready to be selfless in ensuring that she is also satisfied.** Most men are already done when the women are yet to get to the level of satisfaction that they desire. For a woman, her sexual satisfaction is not just in the intercourse, it is in the loving atmosphere created in the home. She must not see the husband as a burden when it comes to the matter of sexual intimacy.

Dag Heward Mills in his book The Model Marriage also spoke in strong terms of the need for the couple to pay attention to understanding each other's uniqueness and desire in the bedroom. The desire of the couples must be to ensure that they both enjoy sexual intimacy the way they both desire. **No one must insist on always having it his or her way, they both must be willing to make sacrifice needed for mutual satisfaction. The couples must also be willing to go extra mile in satisfying each other sexually.** They are not to do things that contradict the plan and purpose of God for sexual enjoyment, but they must be willing to be creative so that they can enjoy themselves maximally. The woman must learn to keep herself clean and the man must always learn to be willing to make her wife happy before the time of having sexual intercourse. The bedroom must be filled with love from time to time if the couple will enjoy marital bliss.

References

1. H. Norman Wright, "So You Are Getting Married", Regal Books (1997) edition; Latter Printing, paperback, 256.

2. Gbile Akanni, "No more Two", Living Seed Media, (2011), 374.

3. Dag Heward Mills, "Model Marriage", Parchment House, (2007), 320.

4. Tim Lahaye "The Act of Marriage", Zondervan Publishing, (1998),400.

5. Myles Munroe, "Understanding The Power and Purpose of a Woman", Whitaker House, (2001).

6. Walter Trobisch, "I Married You", Barnes and Noble, (1971), 168 Pages.

7. Gary Chapman, The Five Love Languages, Moody Press, (1992)

Made in the USA
Columbia, SC
19 June 2021